2020 VISIONS: HEALTH CARE INFORMATION STANDARDS AND TECHNOLOGIES

Based on a September 1992 Conference Sponsored by the United States Pharmacopeial Convention, Inc.

Edited by:
Clement Bezold
Jerome A. Halperin
Jacqueline L. Eng

Published by USPC, 12601 Twinbrook Parkway, Rockville, Maryland 20852.

ISBN 0-913595-72-1

Text printed on recycled, acid-free paper with vegetable-based ink.

Acknowledgements

We acknowledge the contribution of many people to the success of the September 1992 Conference that served as the genesis of this book.

The authors and the reactors provided openness, real dialogue, and insights during the Conference discussions. Science writer Gina Kolata played the role of moderator with interest and enthusiasm and kept the discussion moving and understandable.

The participating scientists, health care policy setters, academicians, and pharmaceutical executives contributed their experience and collective wisdom to help stimulate discussions about our futures.

Suzanne Masica, the Conference's graphic facilitator, added a new dimension of understanding by creating a "visual memory" in real time and coached the small groups in how to draw their own ideal designs. The hand drawn figures in the text are either from Suzanne or from the small groups.

Gail Martin, of Editorial Associates, worked extensively with the authors before and after the meeting to develop the discussion summaries. Institute for Alternative Futures staff members Susanna Palmer, MaryAnn Puglisi, and Kathy Scott and USP's Dorothy Chaconas provided invaluable logistical support for authors and Conference participants.

USP staff members Barbara Bowman, Angela Long, Faye Pannell, and Frances Rampp worked diligently to put together the comprehensive resource that served as the guide for the Conference.

And finally, this book—that allows expansion of the discussions of 60 people to the breadth of the community interested in the future of health care technologies—was brought to life through the editorial and creative talents of USP staff members Patricia Morgenstern, Gail Oring, Tia Morfessis, and Mary Regan.

Contents

Preface

Analytical methodologies . . . *Biotechnology* . . . Cosmeceuticals . . . *Drug interactions* . . . *Efficacy* . . . *Free trade agreements* . . . *Gene therapy* . . . *Health care costs* . . . *International drug development* . . .

Without much difficulty it is possible to identify a new or changing health care issue for each letter of the alphabet. It is within this milieu of change that the United States Pharmacopeial Convention (USP) offers, to all who are interested in what the world of health care technology will look like in the year 2020, this compilation of commissioned papers, discussions, and recommendations.

This book documents a September 1992 Conference, *USP 2020: The Strategic Context of Drug Standards and Drug Information.* The Conference was one element of a series of introspections ongoing within USP to assure that it retains the vitality necessary to address the health care needs of the American Public in a constructive way. This book reflects the perspectives and insights of 60 USP family members and senior executives from the pharmaceutical industry and federal government, representatives of health care practitioners and educators, and patient and consumer advocates who attended the September Conference. These insights already are being used in evaluations of USP membership, governance, and history to assess how well USP is meeting and, in the future can meet, its mission to protect the public health.

In planning the discussions, however, we took great pains to assure that the Conference focus was on the broadest picture of health care technologies. While *USP 2020*, therefore, was convened **by** USP, it was not **about** USP. The year 2020 is a natural target for our organization's strategic planning, as it is the year we shall be celebrating our bicentennial. 20/20 also seemed appropriate as we wanted to focus participants' visions on the design of an optimal system of health care delivery and, in turn, what that optimal system might mean to what we today call the drug standards-setting and drug information development processes.

The results of the Conference should be of special interest to organizations and people working to protect and promote the public health. Only by actively anticipating and planning for our future with openness and willingness to change and adapt to future needs will the health care technologies industry succeed in remaining viable.

We trust that this book stimulates thought, engenders contemplative discussion, and contributes in a positive manner to the vision of the patient-centered health care delivery system that emerged from the Conference. While USP must create and work toward its own vision and implementation strategies, so must its practitioner, educator, industry, and patient partners work toward their visions and strategies. Turning individual visions into a shared vision and into reality will be the true test of whether or not our combined efforts to protect and promote the public health will have been successful.

Rockville, Maryland
April 1993

J.A.H.

Introduction and Summary

This book provides a look to the future—out as far as 2020—for two audiences. The first audience is the community of health care providers, pharmaceutical manufacturers, regulators and other policy makers, who can benefit from taking a long term view of the development of standards and information systems for pharmaceuticals and the health care systems into which those technologies may evolve. The second audience of this book is those people in the above groups who are concerned about the work of the United States Pharmacopeial Convention (USP). USP is the oldest standards-setting organization in the United States, and a leader globally in developing standards and information for pharmaceuticals and related articles. Standards-setting in the current USP context primarily involves establishing and publishing standards on the strength, purity, packaging, and labeling of pharmaceuticals and other articles. Information in this arena for USP currently involves information for health care providers, patients and consumers on the appropriate use of these articles. USP has been providing standards for nearly 175 years. It has been providing information for over 20. USP will be 200 years old in 2020. Will the same functions be necessary? Looking ahead, as the material in this book does, it is entirely possible, even likely, that the nature of pharmaceuticals, and the processes for their development and use will have changed dramatically by 2020. However, there is not a clear picture of how those changes will evolve. Even more important than what is likely are the questions of what should the systems for standards and information for health technologies be? How should they evolve? What role should USP play?

> **"It is entirely possible, even likely, that the nature of pharmaceuticals, and the process for their development and use will have changed dramatically by 2020."**

This book and the Conference it summarizes are an effort to take a creative look into the future, and to provide USP with key insights in its strategic planning, particularly for formulating a vision for its own unique, long-term contribution. The Conference was not intended to develop a vision or a plan for USP; USP must do that in its internal forums. The Conference was intended to take members of the USP family and those beyond USP on a mental reconnaissance mission. For participants at the Conference and for readers in health care, pharmaceuticals, and standards-setting beyond the USP, this material will convey a sense of possibilities and of threats.

The Conference Task and Process

The Conference, *USP 2020: The Strategic Context of Drug Standards and Drug Information*, brought together leaders from medicine, pharmacy, the pharmaceutical industry, government, consumer groups, and health futurists. The group met from September 9–11, 1992 in Annapolis, Maryland. The future environment was summarized in five papers that were presented and discussed. The forecasts in these papers showed the variety of challenges the field will face, particularly from advances in basic knowledge, new therapeutics, delivery systems, the integration of drugs and devices, health care delivery changes, the globalization of manufacturing and commerce, new concepts in the standards field, and powerful advances in the general information infrastructure.

"If you were designing the ideal systems for standards and information for health technologies in 2020, what would they be?"

After reviewing what might happen as outlined in these papers, participants broke into small groups to answer an important, but seldom asked question: If you were designing the ideal systems for standards and information for health technologies in 2020, what would they be? The participants showed that compelling "ideal designs" can be formulated for what the systems should become. Participants developed compelling designs for both standards-setting and information systems that gave USP, and others who will be involved in shaping these systems, much to reflect on.

There was not consensus on how broad USP's role should be. These differences centered over whether the information systems should be designed to ultimately aid patients and consumers or stay focused on improving the standards-setting system primarily supporting professionals. For those in the field, these differences highlight important choices.

The Conference process included two other special features, a science writer to moderate the discussion, and a graphic facilitator to record the results. During the Conference each author briefly summarized his paper and was followed by a panel of experts serving as reactors. To provide additional insights from the perspective of a journalist, these sessions were moderated by *New York Times* science writer, Gina Kolata. In addition, all of the presentations and discussions were summarized by graphic facilitator, Suzanne Masica. This graphic material provided a "visual group memory" as the discussions proceeded and encouraged participants, during the small group sessions, to draw their own ideal designs. The hand-drawn figures in this book come from Suzanne Masica's work and those of the small groups.

The year 2020 was chosen as a focus for the Conference because USP will be 200 years old that year, and the time from the 1990s to 2020 provides a sufficiently challenging time frame for USP's consideration of its long term contribution. For Conference participants the focus on 2020 represented a time far enough into the future that dramatic change could be considered. Many of the forecasts considered here are likely before 2020.

Book Contents

This book includes the five papers developed for the Conference, as well as a summary of the discussions about the papers and about the "ideal designs" developed by the participants. Thus the next six sections cover these topics:

- scenarios for standards and information for health technologies
- the health care delivery system
- health information systems

- medicines and technology
- regulation and standards
- "ideal designs," Conference discussions and conclusions

Alternative Scenarios

To develop overview scenarios for standards and information systems for health technology, Clement Bezold interviewed experts on standards from inside and outside of USP, and added his extensive scenario work from the Institute for Alternative Futures. The resulting scenarios in Chapter 1 see great change even in the extrapolative scenario. In the extrapolative *high technology/continued growth* scenario, standards are necessary for drug-device combinations, including biosensors. These standards are developed for the global marketplace. The *hard times/focused innovation* scenario assumes a frugal, Canadian-like national health care system with basic new technologies routinely developed for mass consumption and more expensive and function-enhancing technologies developed for the privately funded sector. In the *global business* scenario, the need for effective global operations leads to the decline of pharmacopeias because of horizontal standards for all manufactured chemicals, developed globally via ISO, the International Standards Organization, replacing the vertical standards for pharmaceuticals (chemicals for human use). The use of cost-effective drug-device combinations is also a global phenomenon broadening the need for standards. Finally, in *the new social contract* scenario, health care "destandardizes" as diagnoses and therapies are tailored to each biochemically unique individual and include homeopathic medications, bioelectric and behavioral approaches. In this scenario pharmacopeias and related voluntary standards-setting groups take a lead in creating "smarter markets" that provide effective information to consumers and health professionals to compensate for the decline in standardization of health therapies.

> **"In the *new social contract* scenario, health care 'destandardizes' as diagnoses and therapies are tailored to each biochemically unique individual . . ."**

When polled about the likelihood and the preferability of these scenarios, participants said that the hard times scenario was most likely but least preferred, while the social contract scenario was the most preferred and the least likely. While this is understandable, it sets up a dilemma that most organizations share: they reinforce the status quo they don't want because of a failure to explore what futures they want to create, or because of a lack of commitment to bring about their preferred futures.

Health Care Delivery

Leading health futurist, Russell Coile, of the Health Forecasting Group, provided his own image of health care that combined aspects of all four of the scenarios above. In a socially and technologically advanced picture of Health Care in 2020, international cooperation in technology-sharing facilitates truly global standards and networks for communicating relevant information. The emphasis of health care shifts from acute to chronic care and from technology interventions to community health. Capitated care with "social HMO's" facilitate this community health focus among providers.

The use of outcome measures leads to greater consistency of the therapies used globally, and health care systems become more similar, even to the point that a "Euro-med" style of medical practice emerges.

The human genome is mapped, giving rise to the ability to forecast and correct genetically related conditions. Health care moves to "predict and manage" their patients to prevent illness or minimize that which does occur. Prescription use drops in favor of OTCs and better nutrition. Health care service expenditures are capped and public rationing programs emerge to set priorities within the expenditure limits. Nurses and other care givers, including pharmacists, assume greater responsibility.

There was a wide range of opinion among participants, some of whom were not as optimistic that health care would change, that positive value change would take place in the population to support either healthier conditions or improved and more justly financed health care. Others felt that alternative remedies would grow in importance and that outcome measures would ultimately guide health care providers into using the most appropriate therapies.

Health Information Systems

The information infrastructure will see dramatic advances according to Michael McDonald, President of the Windom Health Enterprises. Microprocessors will be as pervasive as plastic. Most of them will "talk" with each other while still doing "the will of humans." They will collectively exhibit "intelligence" far beyond homo sapien capabilities today. Health Oriented Telecommunication (HOT) applications will combine communication, knowledge storage and processing. The synergistic effects of pharmaceuticals, device use, lifestyle, environment, and genetic predispositions within integrated preventive and therapeutic regimens will be built into our personal health information systems and clinical systems. The necessary infrastructure to allow this to be in every home will arise as the definition of "universal service" broadens beyond a simple telephone dial tone to include the emerging interactive multimedia services. Simulated humans and animals will be used for some aspects of new drug/therapy testing.

The capture of outcomes information will not only allow more tailored therapies, but will lead to all clinicians being certified and recertified to perform their treatments on the basis of their simulated or actual performance. The HOT systems will also enable consumers to do far better self care.

> **"Drugs can be designed to be active only within specific tissues, and can be 'manufactured' endogenously, within the body."**

Implanted biochips and nanodevices will maintain biochemical and electrical homeostasis. Drugs can be designed to be active only within specific tissues, and can be "manufactured" endogenously, within the body. Given the changes in pharmaceuticals and information systems, the contribution of standards groups will increasingly shift to decision-support or information-providing activities, rather than the standards-setting itself, and will create and become part of a global standards and regulatory agency that not only provides harmonization, but deals with multidisciplinary issues and accelerates positive developments.

This will be an era of transformative change. Telecognition—the heightened ability to perceive, learn, and understand arising from the interconnection of humanity and interactive media—is the result sought rather than development of simply faster and more powerful information technology.

These forecasts from McDonald raised much discussion, but there was a sense on the part of many, particularly the experts most involved in developing health information applications or systems, that McDonald's forecasts were on target. For example, Donald Bennett, Director of the AMA's Drug Evaluation Unit, generally agrees with McDonald, even McDonald's forecasts that computers will exceed human decision-making capacity in certain areas. Bennett argues that only the computer will be capable of correlating and comparing the massive amounts of data that will be available, particularly data needed to individualize diagnosis and therapy (see Chapter 3).

The discussion also anticipated the later topics, leading to consideration of whether the drug approval process would be speeded up (most thought not radically) or even whether the current drug approval process would be made irrelevant for biochemically unique, endogenous drugs because FDA may not have the authority to regulate them.

Medicines and Technology

In Chapter 4 health technology assessor Stuart Davidson agrees with the earlier forecasts that we will be able to predict, prevent, diagnose, and treat disease at the molecular level. We will have nearly 100% accuracy in diagnosis thanks to new generations of ultrasensitive imagers, biosensors (including DNA chips), and monoclonal antibodies of ever-increasing sensitivity and specificity. As noted, the nature of individualized therapies raises important regulatory and standards questions as these individually tailored medications have not come under FDA regulations.

Davidson points out that pharmaceuticals will increasingly act as packets of information, blocking transmission of deleterious information from genetic sources, blocking cell receptors, and interfering with the signalling pathways inside the cells that lead to the uncontrolled growth of cancer and other diseases. New diseases will arise, but we will be able to quickly identify and control these at the molecular level.

This theme of new technology driving new medications and new concepts of care was reiterated by Gregory Fahy in describing "nanotechnology"—the technology of highly versatile and inexpensive molecular fabrication, molecular manipulation, and molecular-level manufacturing (see Chapter 4). The implications include a shift from the imprecision of today's manufacturing to the continuous sensing of near-flawless production processes. There also will be a shift from today's drug (a single molecule with an often sophisticated but always limited repertoire) to "smart pharmaceuticals" with programmable machines with a range of "sensory," "decision-making," and "effector" capabilities. Smart pharmaceuticals will avoid side effects and allergic reactions through generic, biocompatible housings that are activated only upon reaching their ultimate destinations and attaining almost complete specificity of action. That action might include not one chemical reaction but several, or three or four "sister" agents might be combined into one "smart pharmaceutical."

'Smart pharmaceuticals' (programmable machines with a range of 'sensory,' 'decision making,' and 'effector' capabilities) will avoid side effects and allergic reactions.

The discussion ranged broadly, with many examples of how current experience confirms and refutes the forecasts for more advanced therapies. In addition to these high tech directions, some participants felt that a broader range of therapies, particularly natural and homeopathic remedies, would be more widely used.

There were some concerns for the innovation process raised by the discussion: the pipeline of effective researchers would not be adequate, the economics of more targeted drugs for smaller populations; or even individuals would radically alter how R&D must be done; and that far better information systems will be necessary to deal with both the complexity of therapies, the changes in the medications and devices themselves, as well as the learning from the outcome measures resulting from their use. This last point was addressed in Chapter 6 on ideal designs.

Regulation and Standards

Washington lawyer and former FDA Associate Chief Counsel William Vodra forecast that the core of current regulatory activities will remain, though we are more likely to achieve a clearer distinction between technical and policy matters, with greater reliance on nongovernmental groups such as USP for the technical questions. Also the regulatory function performed by medical, pharmacy and other licensing boards, and by various groups in the marketplace, particularly health care insurers and financing bodies, will remain. Participants generally shared this view, though some felt that with the information systems described above, the new therapeutics would force change in regulation. And more rapid movement from Vodra's cautious and conservative forecast would occur, with the regulatory system changing more radically, if fault and related tort liability questions were changed, and if we reverted to pre-WWII attitudes about death and dying.

> **"The new therapeutics would force change in regulation."**

Standards are likely to be seriously affected by the movement toward process standards (this builds quality into the production process, rather than focusing on screening error out after production as many standards systems now do). As global harmonization leads to compatible but not necessarily identical requirements, inconsistency between European and U.S. regulatory concepts will need to be reconciled, providing an important role for standards organizations.

Anticipating an observation that would arise later, it was noted that standards and information are not likely to remain separate. Information on the use of the standard would increasingly become part of the standards themselves.

Ideal Designs for Standards and Information 2020

Having reviewed and discussed a variety of forecasts, Conference participants formed small groups to develop their ideal designs for the systems for standards and information.

The participants were divided into four small groups. Two groups focused on ideal designs for standards, one on information systems, and the fourth group considered both.

The two groups focusing on standards both saw the ultimate development of international or global systems for standards that were more integrative or inclusive than simply pharmaceuticals. For one group, integrated standards setting would cover health-related software, devices, drugs, and biologics. The second group, focusing on standards, added homeopathic substances, nutriceuticals, and botanicals to the list. Both saw continuous involvement of government and nongovernment agencies, with greater trust and reliance on the nongovernment agencies. A clear, multistep process of standards and regulation by nongovernment agencies, government and the marketplace would evolve, with the degree of standards-setting and regulation dependent on the degree of risk involved in the article or its use (see the "stop-cock" model on page 195). This would more clearly separate technical and scientific functions from political and regulatory ones, relying more heavily on nongovernment groups for the former. Nongovernmental standards-setting groups would also engage in auditing the quality of the data at various points in the multi-step process.

"The health information system would be user friendly for all of its users, whether consumer or health care professional, and operate for users at their particular knowledge level."

The two groups that considered information systems broadened their design to include a wider set of factors and both placed the patient/consumer at the center of the evolving system. Both groups took full advantage of the emerging information infrastructure to gather and provide appropriate information to each level of the health care delivery system. The health information system would be user friendly for all of its users, whether consumer or health care professional, and operate for users at their particular knowledge level. Standards in this context would be expanded to include not only the actual standard but the information necessary to promote the use and recognition of the standard by patients and providers.

There were differences among Conference participants about these designs that raise important questions for those who will shape standards and information for health technologies. Some participants who had focused on the standards role could not understand and did not think it appropriate that USP would concern itself with information systems dealing with the doctor-patient relationship, much less systems that would empower the patient. As noted, those focusing on the ideal systems for information placed the patient at the heart of their ideal systems. Such groups will need to define their own visions for information systems in relation to consumers.

While there was diversity, when asked what they found compelling there was general agreement that the ideal system would: be accessible and universal, empower all participants, produce comprehensive outcome-driven standards that respect individualized treatment, allow risk assessment to guide the degree of standards and regulatory requirements, and have a strong confidentiality capacity.

Conclusion

The materials in this book and the Conference discussions did range from the present out to 2020. And as is often the case, looking to the future is more comfortable and natural for some, the material clearly points out threats and opportunities for those concerned with standards and information for health technologies.

In USP's case, the material here poses important choices, particularly USP's vision for itself and the standards and information field and the way it exercises its leadership to achieve that vision. USP has been the leader in the U.S. for over 170 years in setting standards for medicines. It has taken a leadership role since 1970 in providing information.

Yet between now and 2020 much of USP's core standards-setting activity will face challenges. Take for example the potential that many of the pharmaceutical therapies for which USP develops standards will be augmented or displaced by (1) combinations of current drugs and device/information combinations, (2) molecular level therapies which are tailored to the individual, and not amenable to mass standards, (3) molecular level fabrication of therapies in the body—smart pharmaceuticals or pharmaceutical/clinical laboratories which circulate in the body and activate/manufacture their product when appropriate. These pose both threats and opportunities. Likewise horizontal standards for all chemicals, based on process standards, would eliminate the need for much of USP's current efforts even while it poses new opportunities.

Likewise the material here, particularly the ideal designs, puts forth systems that will be a stretch from our current reality. For example, creating a truly global system of standards and information that is accessible, empowering to all participants, and improves public health and welfare will take serious leadership, particularly since most national pharmacopeias have a limited focus on reference standards for medicines to serve health care professionals and manufacturers.

Lessons from the public and the private sectors show that when confronted with as challenging a future environment as this some groups are paralyzed. Others, particularly those that articulate a powerful shared vision, are able to forge ahead, even if it means transforming the system. At this point it is important that the community concerned with standards and information for health technology press ahead to develop its vision in the context of the longer term future presented here.

1

Scenarios: Setting the Stage

by Clement Bezold, Ph.D.
Institute for Alternative Futures
*Alexandria, Virginia**

In 2020, the United States Pharmacopeial Convention (USP), the oldest voluntary standards-setting organization in the United States, will celebrate its bicentennial. The USP has organized this conference, *The Strategic Context of Drug Standards and Drug Information,* in an effort to take a thoughtful and creative look into the future. The Conference will provide the USP with key insights to carry out its strategic planning, particularly its search for its own unique, long-term contributions. In addition, the Conference record will become a major resource for the pharmaceutical, health care, and standards-setting communities as they explore the decades ahead.

The role of the USP has diversified since its founding in 1820. At that time, physicians generally performed the functions of researching, manufacturing, distributing, storing, prescribing, and dispensing pharmaceuticals. A group of physicians founded the USP to ensure the uniformity of the ingredients that they were using in compounding medications for their patients. The initial purpose of providing standards that deal with the strength, purity, packaging, and labeling of pharmaceuticals remains a major function of the USP. In this century, however, particularly since World War II, drugs that are manufactured,

---

rather than compounded in the pharmacy, have made up increasingly larger proportions of the pharmaceutical market. In 1970, the USP added to each drug's description a paragraph on the use of the drug so that dispensers would have more information to give to their patients and customers. By 1980, the volume of this USP drug information was published separately as *USP Dispensing Information* in parallel compilations, one for health care professionals and one for consumers. Now the USP not only is the principal provider of reference standards for pharmaceuticals and related articles, but also is a preeminent provider of information to health care providers and to patients and consumers on the proper use of pharmaceuticals. In addition, the USP has begun to develop selected standards for certain medical devices used in the human body and has made a major commitment to develop standards for nutritional products (e.g., vitamins, minerals, and related supplements).

The environmental forces that affect the continuing evolution of the USP will be explored in four major papers written for this Conference on drug regulation and standards, the future of health care, drugs and health technologies, and health information systems, as well as in the four scenarios presented here. Between now and 2020, the USP may respond to changes in its environment by expanding its activities to include the provision of standards for drug-device combinations (e.g., biosensors or biocontrollers), standards for the expert systems that will drive much therapy, and standards for and content of advanced information devices that will inform and motivate consumers about their health and therapeutic regimens. The scope of the USP's setting of standards and dissemination of information may grow beyond pharmaceuticals and nutritional products to encompass alternative or nonconventional remedies and legal performance- or appearance-enhancing articles (i.e., cosmeceuticals). Alternatively, automation of the processes by which drugs, devices, and related materials are tested, manufactured, and marketed may reduce the need for traditional, product-oriented standards. Likewise, greater international cooperation and coordination may reduce the role of national pharmacopeias.

As the USP looks ahead, a number of key forces will reshape the need for and use of pharmaceuticals and devices and the corresponding need for standards and information relating to their quality and use.

The most important forces, which have been taken into consideration in developing the four scenarios presented here, are likely to be:

1. *Globalization.* A global marketplace will raise opportunities for international harmonization of drug and technology regulation and standards. "Horizontal standards" (i.e., standards for all products in a general class, such as chemicals, whether or not they are for human use) that are established by voluntary standards groups may reduce the need for pharmacopeial standards for drugs. Competitive market forces and, some would say, good management will create pressures for consistent, if not identical, global standards. These forces could dramatically reduce the role of pharmacopeias or propel them into a new set of functions.
2. *Cost containment and outcomes.* Health care delivery systems are facing strong pressures for cost containment, as well as dramatic advances in therapies. The consistent use of outcome measures to guide medical practice and the related development of high-quality data on the comparative cost-effectiveness of therapies will produce new requirements for drug information and will create a variety of competitors who provide high-quality drug information.
3. *Advanced personalized therapies.* Dramatic advances in biomedical knowledge will lead to new insights about disease processes and variations in diseases and therapies among subgroups in the population, as well as among individuals. The ultimate result, which may occur before 2020, will be a far more personalized therapy in which a knowledge of variations, including genetically based variations, among individuals in their responses to therapy is integrated into medical practice and pharmaceuticals are tailored to these variations. The subsequent new types of drugs and drug "manufacturing" processes will place new challenges on regulatory and standards-setting bodies that have worked to ensure safety and efficacy statistically, that is, on a mass population basis rather than on an individual basis. As health care moves in this direction, new standards will be necessary for the localized "manufacturing" (e.g., on site or in the body) of per-

sonalized drugs and for the information systems that direct their use.

4. *Information infrastructure advances.* Equally dramatic advances will take place in the information structures in homes, offices, and medical care systems as a host of technologies make the environment more intelligent. It will be possible to issue commands to many types of equipment simply by speaking. The necessary and relevant pieces of information for any personal, professional, or medical task (other than the medical records of individuals or proprietary information of businesses) will be available anywhere. In many cases, various electronic media will replace books. Expert systems will augment or supplant human diagnosis and therapeutic selection, including the prescription of drugs and related products. For organizations that have focused primarily on the distribution of printed information, these changes will offer a variety of threats and opportunities.
5. *The predict-and-manage paradigm in health care.* Given advances in biomedical knowledge and advanced information systems, the emphasis of health care will shift from responding to illness after it reaches a certain threshold to minimizing unnecessary morbidity over the course of each person's life. The ability to predict aging and the course of any disease based on genetics, physiological state, and disease history will be combined with advanced therapies that include effective behavior-shaping components.

These forces may dramatically change the environment for standards and information for drugs, devices, diagnostics, nutritionals, and related health care technologies. Yet, because the timing and direction of these forces are uncertain, their precise impact on the environment for standards and information is uncertain. The development of scenarios can serve as a powerful tool in bounding and exploring that uncertainty and in planning for the future. This chapter sets out four scenarios for 2020 that focus on the four principal pathways along which the future may unfold.

Sources for these scenarios include interviews with USP advisors and staff, which yielded a sense of the key forces and the key uncertainties seen from within the organization; interviews with a variety of experts outside the USP; and the resources of the Institute for Alternative Futures (IAF) on health care and pharmaceuticals, including a set of scenarios on twenty-first century health care recently developed for *The Healthcare Forum Journal.*[1] The scenarios will be presented in two forms: first, in narratives that suggest how the future may unfold between the mid-1990s and 2020; second, in a matrix that makes it possible to explore and compare key elements in 2020 across the scenarios (see page 20).

SUMMARIES OF FOUR SCENARIOS FOR 2020

Scenario 1: High Technology/Continued Growth. Technological progress, good management, and a resilient global ecosystem combine to allow economic growth, particularly in the United States. Health care therapeutics advance dramatically. The emphasis of health care is on the prediction and management of illness, which reduces overall morbidity during each person's life course. More personal, focused care evolves through several phases, ultimately focusing on the biochemically unique, DNA-driven variations in health. Drugs and devices (especially biosensors and sophisticated delivery systems) merge with behavior-shaping information. Mutual recognition of much foreign testing expedites the premarket approval process of the Food and Drug Administration (FDA). Standards evolve as drugs, devices, and expert systems merge.

Scenario 2: Hard Times/Focused Innovation. Recurring economic hard times slow growth, but lead to a Canadian-like health care system with a frugal universal basic benefit that utilizes nonphysician health care providers and encourages home care/self-care aided by advanced information systems. The Health Care Financing Administration (HCFA) and the Agency for Health Care Policy and Research merge as cost containment becomes a more significant factor in decisions. A clear two-tier health system emerges in the United States, with roughly 30% of the population buying services beyond the basic benefits. New cost-effective technologies are developed in the publicly funded sector, while more speculative, life-extending, function-enhancing, or cosmetic advances are developed in the privately funded sector.

Scenario 3: Global Business. Because multinational companies are growing, most national economies are also growing. The need for effective global operations leads to horizontal standards for most manufactured items, with the International Standards Organization taking the principal role. In concert with the increasing integration of drugs and devices, horizontal standards for all chemicals eliminate much of the need for separate standards for human use chemicals (e.g., pharmaceuticals) and, consequently, much of the standards-setting function of national pharmacopeias. Drug-device information systems and medical care advances become global in their scope, even in the poorest of nations.

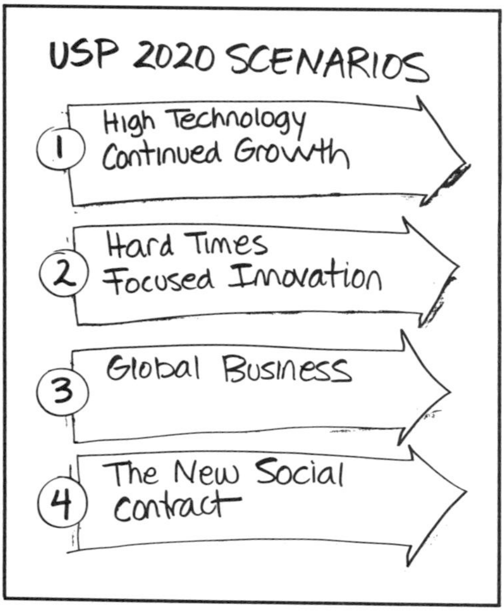

Scenario 4: The New Social Contract. As the social contract (i.e., the exchange of rights/benefits and responsibilities/contributions) becomes more clear and more accepted, and as societies become more diverse, dramatic changes take place in business, health, and health care. Diagnoses and treatments in health care are increasingly varied. Not only is care biochemically unique, but also the treatments include allopathic pharmaceuticals, herbal and homeopathic medications, bioelectric and behavioral approaches. Markets become "smarter" as consumers are more aware of the products and providers that best meet their biochemically unique needs. The nature of standards evolves in this more individualized arena. Sophisticated, ubiquitous, and relatively inexpensive information systems compensate for the lack of standardization. Pharmacopeias, with related voluntary and government information and standards-setting bodies, provide leadership in making the transition to new paradigms for health care and quality assurance.

SCENARIOS

Scenario 1: High Technology/Continued Growth

The three decades leading to 2020 were prosperous, not only in the United States, but also around the world, especially among the developed countries. Some increased environmental protection, combined with the greater than expected resiliency of the earth's ecosystem, prevented serious ecological problems. The countries of Europe successfully united, becoming the world's largest economic unit. The European Economic Community now includes some of the Eastern European and EFTA (largely Scandinavian) countries. In North America, the successful free trade zone between the United States, Mexico, and Canada expanded to include most of the Central and South American countries. Economic growth from the 1990s to 2020 alternated between growth spurts and recessions, but growth was the dominant feature.

Health care delivery advanced dramatically. Although the physician is still the captain of the health care team in the United States and only about 85% of the population has access to health insurance or regular health care, almost all the other components of the health care delivery system evolved. The primary focus of health care expanded to include prediction and prevention of illness, as well as optimal management of disease that does occur. This "predict-and-manage paradigm" enables health care professionals (1) to predict aging and the course of any disease in the individual based on the person's genes, physiological state, and disease history and (2) to prevent or manage disease better through behavioral change and advanced therapies.

The medications and technology that drive the evolving health care system are, by 2020, fully decisive in many cases. The new medicines are based on two major premises. First, although most diseases are multifactorial in their cause and progression, there is usually a fundamental and decisive approach that can prevent or neutralize any disease. For many diseases, the basis of this approach is the recognition that some toxins open up healthy cells at the molecular level for invasion by other toxins, which then cause the damage within the cell. Second, each person is biochemically unique. Therefore, the medicine that stops a particular disease in one person may function slightly differently in another person.

The completion of the human genome mapping project in the 1990s permitted regular forecasts of major diseases in individuals by 2000, and medical practice focused on the biochemically unique nature of each individual by 2010. The new biology provides tools for developing more personalized medicines, which are often "compounded" for the individual by programming the correct instructions into genetic material and directing the distinct genes to grow the appropriately tailored medication. The largely automated "designer gene machines" in clinical laboratories and most pharmacies permit a high degree of quality assurance for this community-based "compounding" of medications.

The ability to prevent the initial penetration of the healthy cell and/or assist the cells and body once the disease process has begun meant an end to most diseases as they were known in the 1990s. For example, cancer, heart disease, and Alzheimer's disease all became curable through pharmaceuticals and sophisticated in-the-body monitors and drug delivery devices. New diseases do arise; once their etiology and pathophysiology have been determined, however, they are quickly and effectively treated.

Closely related to advances in medications have been advances in health-oriented telecommunications. These systems now

- provide continuous, noninvasive (or only minimally invasive) monitoring of each individual;
- feed these data into the person's electronic medical record;
- support the physician by determining how closely the person's current physical and emotional states, as well as disease history, matches his or her genetically predicted health state;
- provide supportive expert systems to assist in diagnosing disease and prescribing therapy;
- provide patients with the appropriate multimedia guidance for understanding their current conditions and their treat-

ment regimens, including their medications (in formats and language that facilitate compliance with treatment regimens);

- encourage patients to shape their behavior in ways that positively affect their health;
- develop health outcome measures for treatments, as well as for physicians and other members of the health care team.

Drugs and health technologies have become much more integrated than they were in the past. To the extent that these drug-device combinations or devices alter the body's metabolic functioning and involve a significant element of potential harm, they have been regulated as drugs. Requirements for substantial evidence of safety and efficacy remain the basis for drug regulation, but better knowledge of disease states and widespread use of advanced information systems in clinical practice make localized trials before marketing approval far easier, quicker, and less expensive than in the 1990s. These same factors, in addition to the improved ability to forecast from smaller numbers of patients, and to capture and provide data to the FDA on the experience of the therapy after it is marketed, have allowed the FDA to require fewer tests or tests on smaller numbers of patients before marketing.

Because of the quality and ubiquity of outcome measurement in medical practice, nearly all clinical uses of a therapy (i.e., a medication, a drug-device combination, or a drug-device combination along with a behavior-shaping information component) have become part of Phase IV testing aimed at more accurately targeting the appropriate patients, tailoring their dosage and reinforcement schedules, and anticipating side effects. Given the movement toward diagnosis, prescription, and compounding of therapies on a biochemically unique basis, these information systems have become essential.

Cooperation and transparency of research protocols and medical practice mean virtually mutual recognition among the FDA and its European and Japanese counterparts. This has lowered the cost and time involved in determining for whom the drug works and in making this information available throughout the developed world. The more affluent countries in the developing world are also tied into this process.

While many Third World countries have joined the ranks of the more affluent Triad countries, most of the poor nations of the 1990s have experienced only slight growth.

> **"Cooperation and transparency of research protocols and medical practice mean virtually mutual recognition among the FDA and its European and Japanese counterparts."**

Standards setting in manufacturing and in many services has been internationalized. Manufacturing process standards have replaced some standards that focused on the qualities of the resulting products. For example, horizontal process standards apply to many types of chemical manufacturing. However, in some particularly critical areas, such as human medications, both the new horizontal standards and the older industry-specific and product-specific standards-setting processes are used.

Changes in pharmaceutical therapy have been dramatic in comparison to the state-of-the-art therapies of the 1990s. Viewed from the perspective of 2020, these changes evolved naturally. In most major lines of therapy, the typical pattern—a crowded therapeutic marketplace in which innovative drugs made marginal changes—persisted until after 2000. By 2000, information systems had developed to the point that any therapeutic regimen in use was no less than 6 months behind the proved state-of-the-art therapy. The cost of new medications in the developed countries put them out of reach for the masses in poorer nations. The masses in poor countries receive cost-effective twentieth century drugs and require the maintenance of twentieth century drug information and standards infrastructure for those regions. While information systems in these countries make it easier for them to develop and maintain their own standards, drug information sources in developed countries have continued to play a role in providing them with information and data gathered decades earlier in the developed countries.

Scenario 2: Hard Times/Focused Innovation

The three decades from 1990 to 2020 saw many years of economic growth, but most young people growing up in this period were likely to have an overall sense of recurring hard times. The structure of the industrial economies was breaking down, yet nothing consistent developed to replace it. Recessions and depressions marked the period.

High unemployment during these decades has led to national job protection strategies in the United States, Japan, and some of the European countries. As a result, governments have found it difficult to cooperate on other matters, and the pace of regulatory harmonization has slowed. The continued globalization of major economic players has proceeded, but at a slower pace in the often protectionist setting. European integration did occur around 2010, but only in the original European Community countries, Russia, and some of the Eastern European nations. Ethnic hostility, repressed by the Soviet Union for 50 years and unleashed in the early 1990s, has persisted and has led to the periodic involvement of the European Community and the United Nations in military operations.

In the United States, high rates of consumption, high energy use, insensitivity to the environment, and a market in which economic forces have taken precedence over questions of fundamental justice have made it impossible to sustain the American way of life. No viable alternative has yet emerged, however. Shifts in the major parties and periodic challenges by third-party candidates for the presidency have contributed little. Unemployment remains high; it has increased between 1990 and 2020 as business owners, whenever they can, use hardware and software to replace workers.

There has been some movement in health care reform. Recognizing the usefulness of the health care system as a target, politicians attacked it. Physicians, hospitals, and insurance companies were the principal targets. The government responded to problems in the health care system by mandating a single-payer system and a very frugal basic benefit plan under which patients generally receive care through nurses and expert systems, often in the home, and require intervention by physicians or the use of expensive technology only infrequently. Innovations that yield cost-effective results within this system are encouraged and subsidized.

As cost-effectiveness became a clear requirement for reimbursement, the Health Care Financing Administration (HCFA) merged with the

Agency for Health Care Policy and Research. The number of alternative therapies available has increased, but the new regulatory agency for approval and provision selects only the least costly as part of the basic benefit. An extensive private health care market provides opportunities for individuals or families to buy services beyond their basic benefits. This private marketplace is also the testing ground for new pharmaceuticals and technologies that are effective, but not necessarily less costly.

Therapy has moved slowly toward more tailored, personalized forms under the universal health care system. Cost-effective information systems are being financed, but research and full incentives for translating genetic and other information into medical practice are often neglected, except on the private health care track. The information revolution has generally increased inequality, allowing the affluent to have access to basic information technologies as much as 10 years before most people do. The single exception to this pattern is in the area of home care/self-care. As low-cost information devices prove capable of dramatically lowering the family's need for health care professionals, these devices are made available.

"Therapy has moved slowly toward more tailored, personalized forms under the universal health care system."

The predict-and-manage paradigm forecast in the early 1990s was fully in place by 2010. Between 1990 and 2010, as the appropriate knowledge was amassed and the frugal benefit plan implemented, the long-term medical cost savings of the predict-and-manage paradigm has made it an essential part of health care.

Scenario 3: Global Business

The three decades between 1990 and 2020 were truly an era of global business. Political tension between the superpowers ended during this period, and, although some conflict between and within countries remains, the military-political aspects of life has become less significant. Economic conflict and cooperation have now become the dominant focus, particularly between the European Community and the North

American Free Trade Zone. The growth of corporations that are global in their scope, ownership, and political commitments mitigates the conflict, however. National governments recognize that, in most cases, these global businesses are the engines for moving society ahead. Thus, when it has been necessary to choose between harmonious functioning of the global economy and protecting national authority, the latter has usually lost.

Early in this period, global businesses targeted a few areas as critical to effective functioning; standards for products were among these areas. The International Standards Organization (ISO) has become the major source of international standards and takes full advantage of the increasingly automated manufacturing systems in applying those standards. A product is deemed to meet standards, for example, if its robotics assembly process determines that its production process complies with the ISO process standards. In many cases, governments enforce these standards.

Horizontal standards specify performance outcomes across similar categories of products (e.g., chemicals) used across several industries. Such standards, which ensure product integrity, would functionally displace compendial standards (e.g., strength, quality, purity, packaging, and labeling). They define active ingredients, products, excipients, and authentic substances. In 2020, the specific product standards that pharmacopeias generated in the past for pharmaceuticals, such as chemicals for human use, are not used nearly as often. Some special standards are still necessary, however, such as those required to establish the safety and efficacy of pharmaceuticals beyond their technical, product-related standards. These safety and efficacy standards are now consistent among developed countries. Furthermore, the testing protocols are such that researchers in one country generally accept data obtained by researchers in other countries. The health information systems in use in all developed countries provide very sophisticated drug information that identifies the patients who will be best served by specific medications.

"Horizontal standards provide process specifications across the manufacturing of similar products. . ."

During the last quarter of the twentieth century, individuals were massed into large populations for well-controlled clinical trials that made it possible to determine the safety and efficacy of new pharmaceuticals on the basis of averages. Under this system, a drug that was a dramatic breakthrough for a small percentage of patients with a particular disease (e.g., 10% to 20%) was not always considered significant or was sometimes more slowly approved than were other drugs. Yet, shortly after the year 2000, advances in medical science permitted biochemically unique treatment for each individual. Therefore, based on the person's DNA "fingerprint," disease history, and current physical state, physicians can now accurately forecast the course of any new disease. They can also accurately simulate the success and side effects of any treatment regimen that they may consider. In the context of biochemically unique care and drug compounding, however, the new regulatory approaches cannot ensure complete safety. This leaves a greater role for consumer/patient decision making and monitoring.

"In the context of biochemically unique care and drug compounding, the new regulatory approaches cannot ensure complete safety. This leaves a greater role for consumer/patient decision making and monitoring."

The new drug regulatory scheme that has emerged in all developed countries allows earlier experimentation with new medications, albeit only after successful results have been shown through "virtual reality" simulations. In this approach, regulatory bodies accept fewer studies and subjects before approving new drugs for clinical use and look closely at the patterns of effectiveness and side effects of the drug in practice. Health care providers regularly capture their experience with the drug in practice as part of their normal information systems, thus reducing the cost of developing many classes of drugs and related devices. The FDA and its counterparts in the European Community and Japan focus less on pre-marketing constraints and more on quality control and oversight of the expert systems used in these production processes and therapeutic encounters, analysis of the massive data influx to determine emerging patterns, and communication of the findings to health care professionals and consumers.

Medical care has advanced in all countries. Although a great deal of variation remains among and within cultures and nations, information systems have done much to make the quality of care consistent. The best practices are rapidly disseminated through the use of electronic systems. Poor nations in developing regions have advanced more slowly, again, with wide variation within and among them. Overall, however, even in poor villages, health care has improved.

Scenario 4: The New Social Contract

The United States of 2020, with its 61 states, is quite different from the United States of 1990. The chaotic decade of the 1990s reinforced the fact that the nation is a diverse collection of races, cultures, and creeds. Yet the 1990s also saw the vast majority of U.S. citizens recommit themselves to enhanced social justice and to the environment. Within the old "lower 48" states, California split into three states in the late 1990s, and the District of Columbia became a state in time for the 1998 elections. Outside the old boundaries of the United States, the success of the separatists in Quebec led to the breakup of Canada, with the Maritime Provinces, the Plains Provinces, and British Columbia joining the United States. In 2020, Quebec remains staunchly independent, while Ontario is leaning toward joining the United States. Similarly, Hispanic territories with strong family and political ties to the United States, particularly Puerto Rico, Cuba, El Salvador, Nicaragua, and Panama, had all become states by 2015. The U.S. capacity to "reinvent" the American dream in a multiethnic and multiracial setting (this time less exclusively European) was part of the country's success as it entered the twenty-first century.

Since a series of climatic changes and several natural disasters in the 1990s were tied to human pollution, pronounced changes have taken place in environmental policy, in public attitudes and behavior toward the environment, and in business and industrial pollution levels. The United States and other developed countries had sincerely accepted sustainable development (i.e., growth that maintains long-term environmental quality) as their national policy by 2000. Consequently, an "industrial ecology" has evolved in which virtually all components of manufacturing processes are recycled; this policy affects standards for products and their manufacture, distribution, packaging, and disposal. In the marketplace, consumer acceptance of the "green" characteristics of products means that several consumer groups monitor the quality of these technical standards and use them in their product ratings. The expert systems, which consumers in most U.S. households now use to determine their product choices and to shop most effectively, incorporate these green ratings. Because of the diversity of consumer needs, many "shades of green" have emerged and are reflected in the ratings. The net effect on manufacturing has been to accelerate the move toward ecologically benign processes and their measurement.

Social idealism reappeared in the 1990s in ways that repeated the social idealism and progressive policies of the 1900s, 1930s, and 1960s. Riots in the early 1990s in Los Angeles and elsewhere made it clear that social problems had to be resolved. The solutions put in place in the 1990s, which relied largely on self-help and community help, proved to be more effective and more enduring that those attempted in previous decades. Some new federal programs were developed, but the huge federal budget deficits limited spending in this area. In the health care area, solutions focused on both community health and reforms that empowered consumers, typically stressing self-reliance, self-esteem, and effective community economics.

Health care delivery has been altered by several factors, including

- biochemically unique medicine, which focuses not only on genetic proclivities and personal history, but also on the learning styles, cultural context, and value choices of each individual that are all important in selecting the appropriate therapy from the more diverse set of therapies;
- a broader armamentarium of truly decisive prevention and treatment technologies, including allopathic pharmaceuticals, herbal and homeopathic medications, bioelectric and behavioral approaches;
- health care delivery by providers who, in most cases, are licensed and relicensed on the basis of their outcomes and whose health care approaches empower individuals to engage in as much effective self-care as possible;
- health care providers who take responsibility for the outcomes of their therapies and share responsibility for the health status of their communities.

Drug regulation moved into a new era around 2000. The Food, Drug and Cosmetic Act of the twentieth century was a classic example of industrial era regulation, particularly in its 1938 and 1962 amendments. At that time, the FDA guarded the public by allowing on the market only those drugs proved to be safe and effective through adequate and well-controlled studies. Thus, the federal government could guarantee the greatest benefit for the largest number, based on a mass standard. In the 1980s and 1990s, this approach was challenged, especially for AIDS and cancer medications. Consumers were more willing to share the risk, particularly when life-threatening diseases were involved.

"Regulators now concentrate most of their efforts on ensuring that consumers and health care providers adequately understand the full range of risks and benefits."

The evolution of biochemically unique medicines has created a serious conceptual dilemma for drug regulation. Safety and efficacy have become more clearly an individual matter that depends on genetics, current health status, past diseases, and other comorbid factors such as personal outlook and stress. Because the FDA and its counterparts in other countries have helped shape a smarter market in which consumers can better judge various therapies, regulatory bodies have shifted their focus. They still protect the public from unsafe drugs, but they share that role with patient and consumer groups. Regulators now concentrate most of their efforts on ensuring that consumers and health care providers adequately understand the full range of risks and benefits.

By the late 1990s, medical informatics, community trials, and more assertive health care providers had fragmented the market for pharmaceuticals by identifying the specific drugs that would most effectively treat particular subgroups in the population. What the FDA had previously looked on as "data dredging" or meta analysis (i.e., reviewing clinical trial data for therapeutic variations related to patient characteristics) had become an important part of regulation. After 2000, as scientists mapped the human genome and codified the capacity to understand and treat disease on the basis of genetic differences, and as an individual's DNA fingerprint became part of his or her medical record, therapy could truly focus on each individual as biochemically unique. By 2010, this was common health care practice.

Health information systems were helpful in managing this complexity. They also allowed individuals to embed their values for health care practice, their concerns for the environmental impact of therapies, and their personal cost constraints into the algorithms for choosing therapies and providers. Even before 2000, these algorithms made it possible to predict with a high degree of accuracy the therapy that was likely to be successful for subgroups of patients. Those became more individualized after 2005.

The FDA and Congress agreed that the FDA's role should be (1) to monitor the systems that generate outcome measures for pharmaceuticals and other therapies and (2) to ensure that vendors appropriately label, market, and communicate information about their products. Long before 2005, most prescriptions for pharmaceuticals were combined with prescriptions for diet and exercise; furthermore, they were accompanied by powerful information devices tailored to reinforce the individual's implementation of his or her health protocol. Medications were often dispensed by means of wristwatch-type devices that monitor the body and automatically provide the appropriate doses through the skin. The greater complexity of drug-technology combinations has been mirrored in the expansion of therapeutic modalities, as nonconventional homeopathy and acupuncture approaches compete with relatively new bioelectric therapies. The FDA has relied on the market to monitor, evaluate, and communicate information about therapeutic risks and benefits. In response, local consumer groups regularly pool data from the electronic medical records of their members in order to monitor and compare the outcomes of local health care providers and therapies used in the community.

Standards setting has generally followed the trend toward automated manufacturing, greater environmental protection, and industrial ecology, by focusing on process standards. This approach has hastened the movement toward horizontal standards—all products of a particular class, such as chemicals, have similar standards, regardless of their application (i.e., whether in manufacturing or in health care).

In the era of a new social contract, pharmacopeias not only provide leadership in developing the guidelines and standards for information systems that allow effective consumer choice in a "destandardized, demassified era," but also play a role in the monitoring systems that link the degree of pollution, resource use, and corporate behavior to specific products. As a result, consumers apply their own values to their product and therapy choices.

DISCUSSION SUMMARY

The scenarios set the stage for the subsequent discussions. Participants were asked to vote on the likelihood and the preferability of the four scenarios. The Conference participants considered the hard times scenario the most likely and least preferred scenario, while they considered the new social contract scenario the least likely and the most preferred. The significance of this result lies in the fact that most organizations plan for the future that they believe to be most likely. The task for organizations is to identify what they want to create, then examine the present strategic context and determine how best to achieve their most preferred future.

The scenarios and the poll on them set the stage for Conference participants to consider their own ideal design for health information and standards.

NOTE

1. C. Bezold, "Five Futures," *The Healthcare Forum Journal* 35, no. 3(1992):29–41.

USP 2020: The Strategic Context—Alternative Scenarios

Scenarios / Elements	1. High Technology/ Continued Growth	2. Hard Times	3. Global Business	4. New Social Contract
Key social and economic changes	Successful growth, continuation of social tensions	Economic hard times, political turmoil, environmental disasters, economic protectionism	High growth, favoring large global firms; increase in social programs and public support to European levels	Sustainable development with greater justice and environmental concern, leading to growth and new products
Health care delivery	Technological advances; unequal distribution of health care resources and innovation; no major national health care reform; large number uninsured; care still fundamentally biomedical in its focus	Canadian style, single payer, with frugal basic benefits; 30% buy up in private system with more technology	Sophisticated and integrated systems of competitive providers; technological advances; financing through tax-based insurance system, with few remaining uninsured	Sophisticated advances in hard and "soft" technology integrated into biomedical, behavioral, and environmental approaches to care; networks of providers who enhance self-care; progressively financed national health insurance
The predict-and-manage paradigm	Yes, a core part of care for those with health insurance or health care by 2000	Yes, a core part of frugal benefit plan by 2010	Yes, a core part of care for nearly all by 2005	Yes, though with greater complexity, broader array of therapeutic schools, and support for higher degree of self-care
Therapeutic targeting	Therapeutic subgroups common focus of therapy by 2000, based on clinical trial data and outcomes research	Yes, though slower in publicly funded care; same in private care market	Therapeutic subgroups common focus of therapy by 2000, based on clinical trial data and outcomes research	Therapeutic subgroups common focus of therapy by 2000, based on clinical trial data and outcomes research; greater psychological grouping

Biochemically unique care, including use of genetic variation	For most people with health care between 2005 and 2010	By 2015 in therapeutic areas where there is clear cost-effectiveness; in private market by 2005	For most people between 2005 and 2010	Yes, with learning style and behavior variation included
Health information systems	Electronic medical record, including DNA fingerprint; outcome measures to identify results and guide innovation; expert systems that decentralize expertise	In basic public benefit care, slow movement to full systems, except where shown to be cost-effective; extensive systems in private sector	Electronic medical record including DNA fingerprint; outcome measures to identify results and guide innovation; expert systems that decentralize expertise	Same as in Global Business, with greater support for self-care and broader array of therapeutic approaches
Health information providers	Therapeutic outcomes generated by health care providers; pharmaceutical device outcomes compared by a few competing groups; USP allies with providers, consumer groups, and the AMA	Outcomes generated by providers; new FDA/HCFA agency responsible for comparing pharmaceuticals and devices; private sector competitors involved in more targeted comparisons	Outcomes generated by providers; pharmaceutical outcomes compared globally by several large employers turned data vendors, and by partnership of USP and other major pharmacopeias with national medical societies	Outcomes generated by providers; pharmaceutical outcomes compared globally by several large employers turned data vendors, and by partnership of USP and other major pharmacopeias, with national medical societies, and with consumer groups

USP 2020: The Strategic Context—Alternative Scenarios

Scenarios / Elements	1. High Technology/ Continued Growth	2. Hard Times	3. Global Business	4. New Social Contract
Medicines and health technologies	Dramatic advances for most diseases; blurring of chemical and electrical therapies; combination of medicines and powerful behavioral information; medicines/technologies and information personalized for most conditions	Advances for major diseases in public sector care where cost-effective; more rapid in the private sector	Dramatic advances for most diseases; blurring of chemical and electrical therapies; combination of medicines and more powerful information common; medicines/ combinations personalized for most conditions	Same as in Global Business, with greater range of therapeutic approaches and combinations
Function-enhancing technologies	Acceptance of manipulating personal chemistry for function enhancement and entertainment leads to major products by 2005	Limited importance beyond private market; or low-cost OTC products	Important products available globally in affluent countries by 2005	Important products, often used with nonpharmacologic enhancements to functioning (e.g., meditation, mental programming)
Health care technology regulation	Cooperating national systems focus on pre-release evidence of safety and efficacy on mass basis; better knowledge, technology, and post-marketing surveillance lower costs	Similar requirements as in High Technology/Continued Growth, though private market encouraged as R&D site for all but clearly cost-effective drug candidates	Globally harmonized systems, focused more heavily on post-release checking of effects	New paradigm, greater reliance on consumer judgment of risks/judgment and Phase IV data; dramatic changes in "prescription" requirements as FDA guarantees less safety; support systems for consumers and providers to make more effective choices

Safety and efficacy standards	Similar Phase I and II requirements, though more efficiently achieved; smaller Phase III, with greatly enhanced Phase IV as part of normal medical practice	Similar to High Technology/Continued Growth though private market encouraged as R&D site for all but clearly cost-effective drug candidates	Similar to High Technology/Continued Growth with global standards emerging by 2010	Because of global information systems, smarter markets, and individualized therapy, alterations in classic pre-marketing approval method; much less pre-clearance by FDA, but quality control on the information systems
New regulatory paradigms, because of more personalized therapy	Slow evolution, with FDA letting medical practice take the lead	New framework developed by FDA to ensure greater cost-effectiveness by better targeting of patients for whom the drugs can be effective	Harmonization of information systems that allow consumers/patients to make more effective judgments	Recognition by laws and FDA that drug/therapy user is the risk taker and move to give consumers much greater choice and risk information; less pre-clearance effort by FDA, but more quality control on the information systems

USP 2020: The Strategic Context—Alternative Scenarios

Scenarios Elements	1. High Technology/ Continued Growth	2. Hard Times	3. Global Business	4. New Social Contract
Standards setting ■ **Product standards vs. process standards** ■ **Horizontal vs. vertical standards** ■ **Standards developers**	Product standards still common on remaining mass market drugs; process standards more common on subgroup and individualized therapies; horizontal and vertical standards co-exist Pharmacopeias and regulatory agencies working more closely; USP an important source for standards for in vivo devices and drug-device combinations	Persistence of product standards and process standards; vertical standards secure Pharmacopeias role for public market drugs and devices; pharmacopeias and manufacturers developing standards for private market drugs	Process and horizontal standards most important; few vertical standards remaining Multinational drug/device manufacturers, a global coalition of regulatory agencies and pharmacopeias, and standards-setting bodies, and regulatory agency setting standards for more concentrated global industry	Process and horizontal standards in use for pharmaceuticals, devices, and nonconventional therapies Voluntary and governmental compendia linked with manufacturers; integration of standards for range of individually tailored therapies

2

Health Care 2020: A Long-Range Forecast

by Russell C. Coile, Jr., M.B.A.
Health Forecasting Group
Santa Clarita, California

Scientific advances and global peace provide an environment that makes health care universally accessible around the world. International cooperation facilitates the development of standards for health care technologies and the establishment of a shared information base for the formation of a truly global network. Health care's emphasis shifts from acute to chronic care, and from technology interventions to community health.

The "global revolution" in health care takes place in an entirely evolutionary manner. Because of the inherent conservatism of medicine, the pace of change is measured, rather than breathless. Limitations in the resources for health care, requiring rationing of expensive technologies even with the development of a resurgent global economy, also slow the pace of change. Three phases of change in society affect the U.S. and world health care systems in three decades of change: 1990–2000, 2001–2010, and 2011–2020.

New World Order: 1990–2000

In the last decade of the twentieth century, a new world order emerges. The peace and stability of the new order make possible global economic recovery from the recession of 1990–1992 and promise long-term economic growth that benefits many nations. In the United States, Congress finally enacts national health insurance, funded primarily by employers and implemented by competing multi-service managed care plans (i.e., social health maintenance organizations [HMOs]). As the former Socialist countries stabilize, most join the European Community; they focus on economic development and basic public health measures to revive their populations. The United Kingdom, Germany, and the Scandinavian countries introduce market reforms to make their national health systems more responsive to consumer demands. Japan promotes economic and human development in Asia. Conditions in many underdeveloped areas worsen, especially in sub-Saharan Africa, Pakistan, the Philippines, and Thailand where the decimation of their populations by acquired immunodeficiency syndrome (AIDS) leaves their national governments and infrastructures badly eroded. World Health Organization (WHO) resources are stretched thin, as WHO attempts to assist in AIDS prevention while investing in basic environmental health measures in the underdeveloped countries.

Health care delivery is voluntarily standardized through the wide acceptance of protocols to manage patients according to professionally defined guidelines that are based on research into clinical efficiency (cost) and outcomes (quality). A body of practice guidelines covers all major diagnoses and procedures by the year 2000. In the United States, the Joint Commission on Accreditation of Healthcare Organizations adopts standards for the top 100 diagnoses as accreditation requirements. Because tort reform puts limits on awards and legal fees, defensive medicine gradually eases. Following practice guidelines becomes a legally accepted defense against malpractice. The easing of the malpractice situation lowers legal and professional barriers to more flexible use of nursing and allied health care workers in patient care and education.

> **"A body of practice guidelines covers all major diagnoses and procedures by the year 2000."**

Technology remains a major emphasis of medicine in the United States, but there is growing recognition of the value of disease prevention, health promotion, and self-care. With everyone covered by managed care plans, the profit incentive shifts from the widespread use of technology as a magnet for new revenues to the cost-effective use of technology to promote health and quality of life. The managed care systems decrease excess capacity, eliminating underused beds and equipment, to reduce overhead and stay competitive. Health plans become aware of community health issues and launch pilot projects in health improvement.

Chronology of Events: 1990–2000

- Health care becomes one of the top three public issues for the 1992 presidential campaign.
- The United Kingdom launches a series of market reforms to shorten queues and give general practitioners and hospitals more autonomy from centralized government control.
- Newly elected U.S. President Bill Clinton and a Democratic Congress enact national health insurance to require all employers to provide basic health care coverage, including drug benefits, to all U.S. workers; legislation becomes effective in 1995.
- Health spending in the United States reaches 13% of the gross national product; expenditures reach more than $1 trillion per year.
- Medicare announces a policy of enrolling all beneficiaries in HMOs before the year 2000.
- The Food and Drug Administration merges with the Agency for Health Care Policy and Research, creating a new national organization, the National Health Protection Agency.
- A National Health Care Outcomes Data Bank integrates the databases of Medicare, private insurers, and managed care plans to provide information for outcomes research and testing of new drugs and devices.
- More than 50% of all first-year medical students in the United States are women.
- WHO announces that AIDS patients number 50 million worldwide; no cure or vaccine for AIDS is yet available.

- Global competition and falling drug prices result in massive consolidation among pharmaceutical manufacturers; ultimately, there are 10 truly global companies (6 U.S., 3 European, 1 Japanese) with 85% world market share.

Impact on Health Care: 1990–2000

Social and Economic Changes. It is a mixed growth, slow recovery scenario for the 1990s, as the United States and Japan regain economic momentum from the recession of 1990–1992 and Europe helps a staggering Russia and the former Soviet states to regain social and economic stability. Global peace makes possible an end to world hunger, and a slow renewal of economic expansion ripples around the globe.

Health Care Delivery. The United States adopts national health insurance, but places limits ("caps") on hospital and physician expenditures. Japan and Canada institute controls to slow the rise in health spending. In Europe, the United Kingdom, Germany, and the Scandinavian countries introduce market reforms to make health services more responsive to consumer demands. Other industrialized nations adopt the U.S. model of "community care networks" (integrated health care systems) to rationalize health care delivery. In partnership with large multispecialty groups, these regional systems contract for care to thousands of enrollees ("covered lives"). Providers in the managed care plans are reviewed on explicit quality and cost standards (i.e., practice guidelines) and are rewarded financially for the clinical competence and cost-effectiveness of their care. Toward the end of the decade (1998–2000), data on the quality of U.S. hospital, physician, and pharmacy services become publicly available on a national basis.

Predict-and-Manage Paradigm. A knowledge of disease processes, aging, and variations among population subgroups improves the ability of health care providers to predict an individual's likely health status (and onset of illnesses). Health care's emphasis begins to shift toward predicting, preventing, and better managing morbidity. At the genetic level, early results from the human genome mapping project begin to pay off by the late 1990s. Decoding the genetic map launches a sequence of medical breakthroughs via genetic therapy for single-factor inherited diseases. Treatments are still experimental by the year 2000, but costs are slowly decreasing and the benefits of genetic research may be available to the general public in the twenty-first century.

Therapeutic Targeting. With data from large patient populations readily available in the late 1990s, it becomes common to direct specialized therapy and outcomes research toward subpopulations with high-visibility health problems, such as breast cancer, prostate disease, hypertension, and dementia (e.g., Alzheimer's disease). These initiatives are multinational, often led by coalitions of multinational pharmaceutical companies and large national health care providers, such as Medicare, the Kaiser Permanente Health Plan, and Blue Cross/Blue Shield. Experiments in therapeutic targeting are initiated in the United States, Japan, and most countries of the European Community, but are too expensive to extend to lesser developed countries.

Health Information Systems. In the 1990s, health information systems expand at a moderate pace, but few reach the goal of being paperless. Health information systems are most highly evolved among regional health care systems in the United States, where providers need information in real time to manage costs and quality. By the end of the decade, most European countries have national health information systems that link hospitals, doctors' offices, and health authorities.

Health Information Providers. National data banks are still evolving among the industrialized nations by the year 2000. Data are spotty, however, and researchers complain that the publicly managed health information systems are inadequate for comparative research studies on drugs, devices, and treatment outcomes. Regional and national health care providers (e.g., Kaiser, Blue Cross/Blue Shield, and coalitions of insurers) develop aggregate sophisticated databases for private studies.

Medicines. Substantial advances in pharmaceutical development take place in a variety of clinical fields throughout the 1990s. In 1995, in response to a widely reported study by the American Association of Retired Persons (AARP) that showed windfall drug profits, Congress establishes a national drug formulary and mandates universal pricing (cost control) that reduces brand name prices by 30% to 50% and generic equivalents by 5% to 15%. Scientific progress continues despite pharmaceutical companies' cutbacks in research and development because of the tough new price controls. Experiments with individualized biotherapeutics make slow progress in the 1990s, owing to high costs and the evolutionary progress of genetic research.

Function-Enhancing Medicines. The medical community slowly accepts the manipulation of physiological chemistry as a legitimate therapeutic intervention to enhance function. The high costs of research and the ethical issues raised by consumer groups in the United States further retard development. European and Japanese drug manufacturers pursue early research, with limited human studies conducted in underdeveloped countries.

Global Cooperation: 2001–2010

As the world becomes accustomed to permanent peace, nations turn to economic and human development concerns. In the United States, government regulations, voluntary adoption of practice guidelines, and cost-competitive premiums among the different managed care plans bring medical care inflation down to 7% to 8%. Overall health care spending continues to rise, however, because of the growing number of elderly in the population. There is significant progress in developing an environmental and public health infrastructure in the remaining underdeveloped nations of Eastern Europe, Africa, Asia, and Latin America.

In Europe, the European Community becomes an established entity, and there is a proposal to combine the national health systems of European Community members into a single "EuroMed" plan to share technology, provide medical education, and purchase pharmaceuticals and devices. The "harmonization" of global standards for pharmaceuticals, medical devices, computers, and software is the first step toward international standardization. The discoveries of a vaccine and cure for AIDS late in the decade spur a worldwide vaccination and treatment campaign. Already, the AIDS death toll has reached 30 million by the year 2000.

The successful completion of the human genome mapping project launches a new era of medicine. Scientists and clinicians begin to practice in the predict-and-manage paradigm, anticipating and treating disease even before symptoms emerge. With 24-hour health information now directly accessible in the home via cable and satellite television, consumers practice healthier life styles. The focus of health care delivery shifts from acute care to disease prevention and health promotion. Consumer use of prescribed pharmaceuticals drops, while over-the-counter drugs and good nutrition wean consumers away from their dependency on prescription pharmaceuticals. The rationing of high-cost health care by managed care plans is controversial, but many plans adopt variations of the "Oregon Plan" to keep costs down. (The Oregon Plan ranks 700 medical procedures and specifically identifies dozens of clinical treatments that are too costly to be reimbursed by Oregon's Medicaid program.) The role of the physician changes from that of team captain to that of consulting expert and supertechnician. Nurses and other care-givers are used in an increasingly wide range of technical and education roles.

Chronology of Events: 2001–2010

- According to Year 2000 census data, fewer than 2 million U.S. citizens are medically uninsured; universal access has been achieved.
- Pharmacists are licensed to prescribe and directly dispense 100 commonly used drugs.
- The U.S. National Health Care Outcomes Data Bank begins to operate in real time, with the concurrent reporting of all patient data by U.S. hospitals and physicians to a central data bank housed at the National Institutes of Health (NIH).
- The human genome mapping project is officially complete; more than 100,000 genes have been identified.
- Genetically engineered pharmaceuticals and biotherapeutics now make up one-third of all drugs sold in the United States and 10% of those sold worldwide.
- The Kaiser Permanente Health Plan reaches an enrollment of 20 million consumers, including 5 million Medicare beneficiaries.
- WHO determines that a new vaccine for AIDS is effective and immediately mass-manufactures it for worldwide distribution.

- Now fully established, the Med-Net computer network links all U.S. hospitals and physicians in an on-line electronic database.
- Congress enacts the National Health Care Practitioners Act, which licenses nurses and specialized technicians to perform 60% of a physician's scope of practice.
- A cure for AIDS is discovered and rushed into worldwide distribution; already 15 million people have died and another 30 million need treatment, but the epidemic is halted.

Impact on Health Care: 2001–2010

Social and Economic Changes. Although the global economy often struggled in the 1990s, the first decade of the new millennium opens with the promise of growth rates of 3% to 4% in the fully industrialized countries and 10% to 15% economic expansion in the lesser developed countries. Investments by the United States, Japan, and Europe in Asia, Africa, and Latin America create jobs and stimulate vigorous growth in local consumer economies. Relative political stability occurs for the first time in recorded history, as the world enjoys continuing peace. Worldwide sales of televisions and videocassette recorders double in a decade as the rest of the world becomes consumers. The distribution of telephones and personal computers becomes almost universal. Electronic technologies merge the telephone, personal computer, and fax machine into a single telecommunications device, called the telecom, which is widely purchased for office networks and home-work communications stations.

"Government controls and 'caps' on spending stabilize health care costs in the United States."

Health Care Delivery. Government controls and "caps" on spending stabilize health care costs in the United States, while market-oriented reforms in Europe, Canada, and Japan reduce waiting times without creating excess demand or inflation. The number of physicians in training declines, but more young physicians enter primary care. With government stipends for medical training in family practice, the ratio of primary care providers to subspecialists rises to 40:60 by the year 2010, an enormous shift from

20:80 in 1990. The scope of their practice is broadly widened so that nurses and specialized technicians can cope with an anticipated physician shortage.

The age of "cookbook medicine" arrives with computerized protocols for all major diagnoses and procedures. The provision of health services is standardized through clinical software and medical work stations. Other industrialized nations emulate the sophisticated regional health care systems (e.g., Kaiser and Blue Cross plans) that emerge in the United States. These managed care plans are responsible for hundreds of thousands of "covered lives" under long-term (3 to 5 year) contracts with large corporations, employer health care purchasing consortia, Medicare, and state Medicaid programs. China and India develop regional health care systems and improve health databases for research and planning. Smaller countries adopt a scaled-down version of health systems development with less technology and more community health care outposts. Lesser developed countries begin to create a basic public and environmental health infrastructure and to upgrade their hospital and community care. For the first time in history, most of the world's population is within 1 to 2 hours of modern medical care. With the virtual elimination of poverty and hunger, major health improvements take place in Africa and Asia.

Predict-and-Manage Paradigm. Regional and national managed care plans begin to implement anticipatory medicine. Health care providers not only emphasize life style changes as the key to health improvement, but also intervene to reduce health threats identified by genetic data. The human genome mapping project is officially declared complete in the year 2008, some 3 years after its originally planned conclusion. The genetic information base for the predict-and-manage paradigm is now 60% to 75% complete. Although there is still much to learn about genetic linkages to illness, the genetic determinants of all single-factor diseases have been identified. Genetic "triggers" have been discovered for a number of common chronic illnesses, including hypertension, diabetes, Alzheimer's disease, high blood cholesterol, and alcoholism. Despite advances, the cause of many cancers has yet to be determined, and investigations are continuing.

Genetically unique care is still considered experimental by insurance companies and government health agencies. A growing number of specialized institutes in the United States, Europe, and Japan make biochemically/genetically unique care available, and wealthy patients from the Middle East and Asia fly to these institutes for the costly treatments. A series of experiments at the National Cancer Institute show promise. The NIH proposes the creation of a broad-scale research program in "bio/gen" care for its budget for Fiscal Year 2011.

Therapeutic Targeting. In the industrialized countries, subgroups are a common focus of therapy by the year 2000. Voluntary support groups for those with particular medical conditions (e.g., AIDS, breast cancer, prostate disease, Alzheimer's disease) collaborate in clinical trials and outcomes research. Consumer groups share data by means of computer bulletin boards. Researchers now track both psychological and physiological outcomes.

Health Information Systems. The Golden Age of universal health information systems finally arrives with the new century. Medicare, private insurers, and managed care plans agree on specifications for a standardized national health information system. The National Health Care Outcomes Data Bank, which is constructed on millions of fully electronic medical records, contains all U.S. hospital and physician data. Some health insurance plans and HMOs have installed home health monitoring stations for their chronically ill patients. All U.S. citizens carry medical "smart cards" with a concise medical history, making the already universal health coverage truly portable across the United States. Comparable efforts under the auspices of the European Community take longer in Europe, but are relatively complete by the year 2010.

> **"Medicare, private insurers, and managed care plans agree on specifications for a standardized national health information system."**

Health Information Providers. Previously private data of pharmaceutical manufacturers, health insurers, and self-insured employers are placed in the National Health Care Outcomes Data Bank. Low-cost access charges allow drug companies, insurers, and employers to compare the efficacy of various drugs and devices. The National Health

Protection Agency and the U.S. Pharmacopeial Convention (USP) use the national data bank for research and standards development. The USP continuously updates health care providers, third-party payors, and consumer support groups on drug and device efficacy.

Medicines. The development of pharmaceuticals and medical devices advances rapidly. In the United States, funding for research and development by pharmaceutical firms slowly returns to 1995 levels. Seeing export potential in medicines, the U.S. government increases funding for basic research at the NIH. Some public/private (i.e., government/ business) partnerships are launched to support promising areas of pharmaceutical research. Biotherapeutics gets more NIH funding. Further consolidation of European- and Japanese-based firms accelerates multinational research efforts in competition with U.S. drug companies.

Function-Enhancing Medicines. The development of function-enhancing medicines continues to proceed slowly, held back by controversy over the approach. A promising stream of research in vision enhancement is an exception. Congress funds a $100 million public/private research and development program in an effort to eliminate the need for glasses and other vision aids by the year 2020.

Global Transformation: 2011–2020

With the elimination of global health threats such as AIDS, the nations of the world have an opportunity to turn toward higher level social objectives (e.g., literacy, environmental improvement, and technological innovation). Health levels rise in Africa, Asia, and around the world, as AIDS comes under control. Medical technology's emphasis shifts from restorative care to function enhancement. Neurological implants assist the disabled. Genetic diagnoses and artificial intelligence support a predict-and-manage paradigm in medicine, extending the quality of life. The role of nutrition is widely recognized in supporting health and life quality.

European consolidation results in the adoption of EuroMed, a multinational health system that shares expensive technology and medical specialists. In the 1990s, most authorities believed that it would never be possible to establish such a health system because of cultural differences and variations in medical training and practice. Yet, 15 years after European economic unification, medical "Eurofication" is taking place, and comparative studies of clinical outcomes are leading to the development of EuroMed practice guidelines. By 2015, EuroMed covers the Eastern European countries of the former Soviet Union.

In the United States, coping with the "age explosion" becomes the nation's leading health priority. Beginning in 2011, more than 1 million Baby Boomers reach age 65 each year. Health care plans focus on maintaining the health of the elderly and minimizing the resort to costly technologies. The public now accepts rationing of high-cost technologies. The high cost of dying is falling, as hospice is widely used; fewer than 25% of the elderly die in hospitals. To fill the gaps in medical care availability caused by the decline in the number of physicians, nurses and specialized technicians have a broader scope of practice and receive wages that equal 60% to 75% of a physician's average salary. "Telecomputers," which integrate telephone, computer, and fax machine, are widely available and link the home and the health plan/provider for continuous health information and monitoring.

Chronology of Events: 2011–2020

- A consortium of Johnson & Johnson, Merck, and Burroughs Wellcome establish the first permanent pharmaceutical factory in low Earth orbit at 220 miles above the planet.
- WHO launches Health One, a global health education channel with 24-hour programming available to 500 million television sets worldwide via satellite and local broadcast in 75 languages.
- The United States, Canada, Mexico, and every Central American country except Cuba agree to develop a joint "AmeriPlan," a multinational cooperative health system that is to operate with funds from government and private employers.
- Genetically engineered pharmaceuticals and biotherapeutics now make up 50% of all drugs prescribed in the United States, Japan, and Europe; they make up 30% worldwide.
- WHO announces that a Year 2020 goal has been met; the life span of every resident of the planet is now predicted to reach

75 years, thanks to the worldwide availability of modern health care.

- Genetically engineered human organs developed by an international research consortium are approved by the National Health Protection Agency for clinical use in the United States; the approval is announced simultaneously in Brussels and Tokyo.
- Automated drug-dispensing devices, monitored and guided by implanted biosensors, are implanted into the 100 millionth patient.
- A new study shows that pharmacists have replaced physicians as the primary source of health information and pharmaceuticals for the health needs of 40% of the population.

Impact on Health Care: 2011–2020

Social and Economic Changes. Global stability promotes a continuing surge of worldwide social and economic development. A worldwide investment in infrastructure (i.e., schools, hospitals, roads, and airports) promotes continued growth. An international coalition of countries that are economically interdependent quickly quells occasional conflicts. Moderate inflation makes capital available for growth. Literacy levels rise, while birth rates fall. International brands proliferate in many products. Service industries expand globally.

Health Care Delivery. The system model of regional health care delivery becomes the global standard, with appropriate local variations. In the United States, consumers choose among competing regional health plans in which primary, secondary, and tertiary care have been rationalized. With excess capacity reduced, hospital occupancy has risen to 85%. Few die in hospitals in the year 2020; 85% of deaths occur at home or in hospices. Consumers take more responsibility for their own health. Elsewhere around the world, EuroMed expands into the former Eastern bloc nations. Health care is widely available in Africa and underdeveloped countries through community health outposts. Health levels rise worldwide.

Health care delivery takes full advantage of the information revolution, with extensive computer networking, telecommunications, and automated health data capture (e.g., biosensors and telemonitors). Expert systems assist in diagnosis, guide robotic surgery, and provide continuous case management of the chronically ill. In-home health monitoring and sophisticated technology are common for the chronically and terminally ill patients. Despite the high level of technology, more selective use of technology and broader acceptance of mortality help keep health cost inflation within 2% to 3% of the increased cost of living.

Predict-and-Manage Paradigm. The completion of the human genome mapping project and medical expert systems create the conditions for wide-scale application of the genetic database for the predict-and-manage paradigm in the United States, Europe, and Japan. The costs of genetic testing and computerization slow the worldwide application of the new paradigm, but continuously improving world economic conditions promise to bring much of the rest of the world to this level of health care within another generation.

Therapeutic Targeting. After 2010, therapeutic targeting becomes widely utilized. National and international data banks continuously update information on the efficacy of treatments, drugs, and devices. New drugs and devices are introduced in 50% of the time that product development and approval required in the 1990s. Cost-conscious regional health care systems quickly discard technologies and drugs that are becoming obsolete in favor of newer, more cost-effective equivalents.

Health Information Systems. The health information environment is fully integrated into the home and workplace. Managed care plans monitor their high-risk "covered lives" by means of implanted biosensors and two-way in-home and workplace health counseling/information stations. The linkage of national data banks forms the nucleus of an international database. In this decade, smaller nations will gradually be brought into a global health data bank, now projected for completion by the year 2050.

Health Information Providers. The accessibility of health information for providers increases as the international database becomes a reality. The U.S. National Health Care Outcomes Data Bank now includes all mainstream providers (e.g., hospitals, physicians, and nurses) and some alternate care providers (e.g., homeopaths, acupuncturists, and chiropractors). Pharmaceutical and medical device manufacturers in all countries cooperate with the emerging international health database.

Medicines. Genetic therapies and treatments begin to come to market in broad streams. Genetic care is expensive, however, and many genetic therapies and treatments are still considered "experimental." Personalized drugs and treatments become more widely available, but their costs slow acceptance by U.S. and international health care authorities.

CONCLUSION

The Health Care 2020 scenario envisions a high-health future in which major advances in science are harnessed with socially oriented health systems. Tomorrow's healthy future depends on the ability of key shareholders—providers, consumers, suppliers, purchasers, and government—to form long-term partnerships. The ultimate outcomes of these delivery systems and group cooperatives will be healthy people and healthy communities.

DISCUSSION SUMMARY

Noting that the future is not an accident nor a puzzle to be solved, Russell Coile (President, Health Forecasting Group) described the future as a resource. In that context, organizations can chart a long-range voyage to a preferred scenario. In charting that voyage, the assumptions of organizations and their advisors about the future environment will drive and shape what they believe to be possible and preferable. Because there is no such thing as a future fact, the only way to approach quantification of the future is to

Lacking "future facts," expert opinions help quantify the future.

bring experts together and seek their opinions about what may be and what should be.

In reacting to Coile's presentation, Richard Church (Chief, Pharmacy Program, Indian Health Service) agreed with Coile's approach to the future as something that can be created. At the primary care level, he said, the focus is on people who need help, and the concepts of managed care seem to fit. There is a great need for prevention, however, and the managed care model never has enough resources. Because technology does not always reach them, health care providers at the local level must often be very inventive. It is essential to create a philosophical foundation for the future that takes into account the cultural diversity of patients. With such a foundation, it will be possible to take advantage of technological changes and make appropriate referrals.

Pharmacists are likely to spend less time dispensing medications in the future, Church continued. With the development of new drug delivery systems, the role of pharmacists will expand beyond monitoring disease states, particularly as they relate to drug therapy, to educating patients. This latter task will coincide with the growth of consumerism and the intensification of efforts to prevent disease, both of which will drive the practice of pharmacy.

Stephen Schondelmayer (Professor and Director, PRIME Institute, University of Minnesota) noted that economics are currently driving the health care system, sometimes in undesirable directions. Managed health care systems have been focused on managing budgets, rather than managing the care itself. Managing patient care efficiently and effectively, however, will help to achieve economic goals. In this approach, there will be four basic influences: (1) health care outcomes, (2) technical quality, (3) patient satisfaction, and (4) resource use. Cost containment will be perceived less as a punishment and more as a social responsibility. Comparative information on the effectiveness of drugs and providers will become readily available.

The structure of the health care system is likely to shift within the next 5 to 10 years, according to Schondelmayer. This shift will not necessarily be to a centralized government plan, but to the development of well-defined standard benefit packages that are the only ones to be offered. Providers and insurers will then compete to provide these packages. Developed by a private-public consortium, these packages will provide consumers with a true opportunity to compare prices. Coverage will be the key to managing these standardized benefit packages.

Although technical knowledge will undoubtedly increase, Alan Trachtenberg (Medical Officer, Science Policy and Analysis Branch, National Institute on Drug Abuse) defined the big challenge as crafting social systems to take maximum advantage of that knowledge. For example, the cure for syphilis has been available for 50 years, but the disease has not yet been eradicated.

In a discussion of the possibility that the Food and Drug Administration (FDA) and the Agency for Health Care Policy and Research may merge so that it will be possible to examine not only whether drugs are safe and effective, but also whether they are cost-effective, Coile commented that research in isolation of practice and regulation is a great deal less effective. The market has a role to play in this area. One of the fastest growing fields within pharmacy is managed care pharmacy, and large, effective managed care systems are beginning to perform their own research related to devices and pharmaceuticals. They have already constructed their own formularies and are getting much more involved in the development of practice guidelines and protocols.

"System level standards of care are likely to evolve for at least the 100 most expensive diagnoses and procedures."

System level standards of care are likely to evolve for at least the 100 most expensive diagnoses and procedures. From a public policy perspective, according to Coile, linking this cost:benefit approach to regulation with regard to best practices as well as alternative therapies may be very valuable.

Other participants disagreed with the cost:benefit approach. Carol Marcus (Director, Nuclear Medicine Outpatient Clinic, UCLA Medical Center) commented that the FDA's view of a drug or device may have no correlation with the way that it is used in clinical practice. The FDA may not be interested in the synergistic effect of a drug used with other drugs to produce a particular result and therefore should not be expected to decide the cost-effectiveness of a drug. The marketplace, not the FDA, really determines how a drug will be used. According to Philip Walson (Professor of Pediatrics, Pharmacology, and Pharmacy, The Ohio State University) and Edwin Bransome (Professor of Medicine, Medical College of Georgia), the primary problem may be in defining cost-effectiveness; the definition really requires a definition of clinical effectiveness.

One approach, suggested by Jamie Banks (Senior Associate, Charles River Associates, Inc.), is to consider the market, that is, the type of patient population desired in the future and to determine the cost-effectiveness of a drug, device, or procedure in terms of its usefulness in producing that kind of population. For example, is the population expected to be a relatively healthy, aging population? Has chronic disease been eliminated? With that kind of vision, noted Banks, it may be possible to work backward, placing resources and providing incentives for health care providers to produce the desired type of population. Such a perspective would have an impact on cost-effectiveness. Under the present system, cost-effectiveness may be different things to different providers. Procedures that are cost-effective over 5 years may not be cost-effective in the long term.

A vision for the future can provide a strategy today for setting policy, placing resources, and providing incentives.

Such a shift from an acute care to a chronic care paradigm will take at least 15 to 20 years, according to Coile. It is unlikely to occur until Medicare, for example, becomes a 100% managed care program, because the current episodic and acute care fragmented system puts the emphasis in the wrong direction. Until the economic reality matches the philosophical desire, there will be no real change.

Despite the discussion of individual choice, there was some concern that one level of paternalism will be replaced by another level of paternalism. Grace Monaco (Director, Medical Care Ombudsman Program, Medical Care Management, Inc.) noted that, instead of mandated benefits on the state level, there may be mandated benefits on the federal level. It is important to educate consumers to the distinction between what they want and what they need. With an ability to evaluate various treatments, consumers will be able to play a role in governing the economics of the health care system. The unpredictability of employers, according to Monaco, makes it essential to establish a system of lifetime health care benefits that does not depend on employers who may go out of business and leave their employees with no health insurance. Under such a system, individuals can control their own health care benefits; they can have their own capitation and can select services within certain parameters as their resources allow. Coile noted that the German system is such an individualized system.

John Yarbro (Executive Director, Regional Cancer Center, Memorial Medical Center) commented that prevention efforts do not guarantee cost savings, as knowledge is not always the key to prevention. Furthermore, the physician is not always the best person to provide health information. Medical education should include more on "health care" and ways to bring about behavioral changes in patients and make them part of a kind of medical democracy. Society however, not the physician, has a greater control of patient education to prevent disease.

Louis Lasagna (Dean, Sackler School of Graduate Biomedical Science, Tufts University) proposed a grim scenario. Many developed countries have a graying population that pays lower taxes and uses more medical care. Most are limiting medical expenditures to a certain percentage of gross national product. While there is a finite limit to what can be saved by making the medical system more efficient, there is no limit to technological advances. In view of these facts, rationing of health care may be necessary, possibly done in the marketplace by managed health care plans. Coile responded that he does envision rationing and that the managed care plans will do it within a market context. The choice in the future is likely to be between cost-effectiveness and individual choice, and the balance may see-saw between the two, according to another participant.

Some participants assumed that the U.S. government will not be able to develop a rational policy to manage a problem as complex as health care. Coile agreed, noting that, in his scenario, government does not take over the health care system, but rather basically retreats to the use of market approaches by contracting with managed plans to provide Medicare and Medicaid services.

It is clear that society has greater capabilities than resources. The problem is to make choices. Not everything that is cost-effective is affordable, which complicates the choice. There must be a paradigm shift in basic individual values. For example, life cannot be extended indefinitely, and it may be necessary for society to emphasize the quality of life rather than the extension of life.

Some participants felt that the role of alternative treatments will grow. Trachtenberg suggested that alternatives should fit into the new system in a cost-effective manner. It is necessary to gather data on the effectiveness of alternative therapies before it is possible to determine their cost-effectiveness, but current data are inadequate for such a determination. Willingness to examine alternative therapies is increasing, however. For example, the National Institutes of Health has just established an office for the study of unconventional medical practices. In addition, the National Institute on Drug Abuse is studying acupuncture as a potentially effective treatment for drug addiction. Presumably, alternative therapies, often high-touch and low-technology, will be among the mix of services ultimately available to patients in the health care mix.

Limitations in the supply of health care resources, as exist in the Indian Health Service, tend to give rise to the use of a variety of these resources. Church emphasized that the provider's basic philosophy must be based on an understanding of the patient's value system. More high-cost, high-technology therapies are not always better. Unique within the U.S. health care system, the Indian Health Service emphasizes primary prevention through modification of life styles.

One participant pointed out that the most cost-effective area of health care is in the provision of prenatal care, yet few who are discussing the allocation of resources have focused enough attention on the population of pregnant women. Despite the cost-effectiveness of prenatal care and of vaccinations for children, the absolute cost is a deterrent for many people. Furthermore, these decisions are made for people (e.g., children) who cannot speak for themselves.

Finally, the question was raised, What happens to new ideas when outcomes are codified on the basis of cost-effectiveness? Will an innovative therapy be overlooked because it does not appear sufficiently cost-effective even to be investigated? An effective database is essential for the development of guidelines for outcome measurement.

Decisions made solely on the basis of cost-effectiveness and resource allocation often ignore the well being of the individuals for whom the decisions are made.

3

Health in the Age of Telecognition

by Michael D. McDonald, M.P.H.
Director, Health and Human Ecology Division
Environmental Science and Policy Institute
President, Windom Health Enterprises
Chair, Communications and Computer Applications in Public Health
Berkeley, California

An examination of the circumstances of 30 years ago in relation to those of the present illustrates the uncertainties of looking ahead and making predictions 30 years into the future. Although the 1960s were in many ways a simpler and more optimistic time, they were not without their own challenges. In 1964, for example, the United States thought that signing the Nuclear Test Ban Treaty might thaw the Cold War following the Cuban missile crisis; China joined the nuclear club without agreeing to its rules and went forward with its first nuclear test that year, however. The U.S. government was expending the remains of the public's post–World War II idealistic concept of warfare by enthusiastically entering into the Vietnam War, but it had yet to deal with the drug and sexual revolutions. The citizens of the United States had not seriously confronted the impeachment of a president since Andrew Johnson had been impeached and acquitted in 1868; little did they know that they would again in less than a decade.

In the mid-1960s, the U.S. public and its policy makers were more likely to perceive an energy crisis as something that an aging grandmother experiences in caring for her grandchildren rather than a limit imposed by finite oil reserves or by foreign oil-producing nations. A computer was still a huge contraption that 99% of Americans had never even seen, let alone touched or used. A man on the moon was a mythical creature that appeared in children's stories, ate green cheese, and symbolized the technological promise of the near future. Putting a man on the moon was to be proof that the human race could fulfill any ambition. Medicare, Medicaid, and the War on Poverty were on the drawing board, but had yet to be implemented. They were thought to hold great promise for reducing the suffering of the poor and removing the barriers between the disenfranchised and the American dream.

In the mid-1960s, the U.S. public and its policy makers were likely to perceive an energy crisis as something that an aging grandmother experiences in caring for her grandchildren.

Smallpox had yet to be eradicated. The unanticipated severe birth defects caused by thalidomide had led to its removal from the marketplace and prompted the 1962 Amendments to the Food, Drug and Cosmetic Act, which regulated the introduction of new drugs and the purity of those on the market. Birth control pills had not yet reached broad distribution. The Rolling Stones had not yet described Valium as "mother's little helper." AIDS was another name for nurses in training. Consumers did not think of using Tylenol, let alone paying the price to make it tamper-proof.

Although many of the factors that contributed to the explosive changes in society in the subsequent decades were unclear to the average citizen in the 1960s, one thing was fairly predictable. The pharmaceutical industry was going to grow exponentially in the coming years. In fact, between 1964 and 1969 alone, pharmaceuticals went from $8 billion to $14 billion in annual sales and represented one of the most successful and influential sectors of the economy.

Roughly 15 years ago, the early makings of the now $3 billion industry of interactive communications appeared; today, the industry serves 3 million U.S. users. At the inception of on-line systems, the IBM personal computer did not exist. Until the 1980s, the now $100 billion microcomputer industry was only a sparkle in the eyes of a few venture capitalists. Even many of those who were to profit directly or indirectly in this new industry would have considered preposterous the idea that this type of marketplace would emerge in one decade.

During the almost convulsive shifts in health science, politics, technology, and social conditions over the last 30 years, the U.S. health care system has been fertile ground for the growth of health technologies, standards, and information. The present and coming decades are likely to bring an even greater rate of change. The merging of telecommunications, computers, and video into one interactive medium is likely to be one of the principal catalysts of change. It promises to have a global reach and to democratize the production of knowledge for those who gain access.

Along with the challenges of rapid change come significant opportunities. Leaders unwilling or unable to contemplate change and to redefine their power and resource base dwindle in importance. Outstanding leaders in times of great change develop an understanding of the forces that shape the future, especially those forces that may be perplexing or paradoxical. Industries led by individuals or teams cognizant of future challenges are the ones that most successfully ride, if not harness, the forces of change.

Although uncertainty and surprise are inherent in the study of the future, the tools for looking at the future have never been better. Some things are more easily predicted than are others. For example, barring major war, severe epidemic, ecological catastrophe, or dramatic changes in migration patterns, it is possible to predict with some certainty the number of people who will be in the United States in 2020, their age, and their ethnicity. Similarly, it is possible to estimate the average length of life of subpopulations, based upon the age, genetic background, socioeconomic status, medical history, and life style of the targeted cohort—as well as the primary diseases to which they will be susceptible at different periods of their life cycle.

Predicting the nature of the communication network that will link the functional elements of the health care system in the future is another issue altogether. The level of innovation and change is so great and pervasive that the usual trend analysis would undoubtedly be too conservative. Trend analysis must be associated with communications and computer technologies in common use in demonstration projects, in the laboratory, and on the drawing board today; however, the horizon of the wide diffusion of these technologies is probably less than halfway to the year 2020 milestone. Therefore, for the more distant future, a goal-oriented approach, identifying the easily foreseen side effects may be the best basis for a description of health-oriented telecommunication applications.

Each new technological breakthrough and each significant historical event alters, sometimes in small ways and sometimes in large ways, what is perceived as important.

> The world determines what we can do and what we do determines the world . . . the creation of a new device or systematic domain can have far-reaching significance—it can create new ways of being that did not exist and a framework for actions that would not previously have made sense.[1]

The unpredictable will undoubtedly creep in and alter the path of history in ways that influence the health applications of communications and computers well before the year 2020. There are two great sources of uncertainty: (1) the regulatory influences that depend on the philosophies of those in the White House and Congress regarding investment in research, development, and infrastructure, and (2) the financial and structural commitments by the huge corporate rivals now beginning the fight for control of the intelligent network and its information services marketplace. Given that this emerging marketplace will most likely generate hundreds of billions, if not trillions, of dollars of revenue, these fights may be protracted.

Context of Evolving Health Information Systems

In order to understand the probable evolution of health information systems and their effect on drug and device standards and information, it is necessary to examine the likely context of these evolving systems.

For example, the problems of today's health care system (e.g., runaway cost inflation, 15% to 20% uninsured and an additional 20% underinsured, and demands for improved health status and better quality health care that require new types of service) and the growing health care reform movement will probably lead to significant changes in the delivery of health care.

Ethnic diversity will increase and political landscapes will change. Representative government will be increasingly perceived as insufficient to maintain the public trust in our government and its theoretical underpinnings in the concept of democracy. Participatory governance, facilitated by interactive media that transform every receiver of information into a producer of knowledge, will significantly reinforce the pillars of social policy and bring the public closer to true democracy. As a result, it will be possible to address the problems (e.g., drug abuse, homelessness, teen-age homicide, environmental degradation) that have defied centralized solutions.

"Participatory governance, facilitated by interactive media that transform every receiver of information into a producer of knowledge, will significantly reinforce the pillars of social policy and bring the public closer to true democracy."

The now 5.5 billion human beings will become 11 billion on this relatively small planet within the next 50 years. There will be significant constraints to further insensitive exploitation of the environment. Carrying capacity issues will force a deceleration of population growth. The global consequences of this development will lead to an increased focus on health problems, many of which can only be solved through prevention, and will affect societal perspectives and human behavior from the individual level to the planetary level.

With at least the surface of the Iron Curtain torn down, the differentiation of global telecommunications and markets will accelerate. The world's knowledge, mixed together with live videos and up-to-date statistics of wars, revolutions, and sporting events, will be piped into the home and workplace at astronomical rates. The user's control of the media, speed of information absorption, and ability to produce and disseminate knowledge will be vastly amplified. Telecognition in virtual reality, rather than entertainment, computing, or telecommunications, will be the primary function of the dominant media of the year 2020. The ability to gain immediate access to applicable content, to process knowledge, and to simulate future events in order to optimize human experience and prevent adverse outcomes will replace memorization and simple machine-independent problem solving as the mainstay of education.

Although unification of culture, language, and economies will be a natural outcome of the new dominant interactive multimedia, the simultaneous differentiation of local attributes will strengthen community knowledge bases and community self-determination. Communities, however, will not necessarily be defined in geographical, ethnic, or historical terms as in the past. Virtual communities, a phenomenon of people who spend large amounts of both their leisure time and their work lives with others within the media (cyberspace), will develop naturally on the lines of mutual opportunity, institutional structure, and similar values.

Microprocessors will become as pervasive as plastic. Not only will people wear microprocessors on and in the body, but also they will have these devices in virtually every room and nearly every appliance, as well as in vehicles, purses, and pockets. In many cases, the microprocessors will be vastly more powerful than is any computer in existence today, and most will "talk" with each other without a human intermediary. They will still be doing "the will of human beings," but they will collectively exhibit "intelligence" far beyond their homo sapiens capabilities today—except in realms related to "common sense," heuristics (i.e., rules of judgment), and other uniquely human aspects of intelligence. Computer-assisted decision making will dramatically affect all aspects of human life, including medicine, self-care, public health, and pharmacy.

"Microprocessors will become as pervasive as plastic."

Knowledge reaped from the human genome project and the application of genetic engineering technology will change our perspective on human biology. Many fatal and debilitating diseases untouched by present surgical and pharmaceutical interventions will be resolved—in many cases before clinical manifestations ever become apparent. Little by little, cradle-to-grave monitoring and predict-and-manage intervention with the well individual, mostly outside the clinical setting, will substantially replace the traditional "curative medicine."

Because organic molecules have unique qualities as superconductors, some hypothesize the eventual emergence of "biochips"—biological matter that is programmable. From the far edges of today's science, some glimpse a time when the telecognitor (i.e., an external electronic device that amplifies human cognition) will fuse with human biology. Perhaps, the parallel evolution of computers and molecular biology will merge toward this end around 2020. Perhaps, 2020 will provide only a better historical perch from which to speculate about the barriers to or potential contributions of telecognition and biochip technology. Or, perhaps, 2020 vision—aided by 2020 telecognition—will make it possible to use biological substances, as some propose, to manufacture organic substances and even nanocomputers in the body, as well as in the laboratory, in highly predictable ways to improve physical health and mentation.

"Some glimpse a time when the telecognitor will fuse with human biology."

In summary, given present observable breakthroughs in information technology combined with regulatory changes, consumer interests, and rising corporate competition in the telecommunications and the computer industries, one of the predictable changes of enormous consequence globally will be the development of a ubiquitous intelligent network. Its ramifications for human health are enormous. It offers important solutions to today's health care crisis, and its introduction and maturation over the next few decades will alter the health care system in significant ways.

The increasing complexity and influence of health-oriented telecommunication applications in the years and decades ahead will predicta-

"How will the mandate of today's regulatory and standards-setting institutions change as the boundaries between electronics and chemistry blur?"

bly broaden the role of those institutions involved in the regulation and standardization of health care technologies (e.g., the U.S. Pharmacopeial Convention [USP], the Food and Drug Administration [FDA], International Standards Organization [ISO], the Agency for Health Care Policy and Research [AHCPR], the Health Care Financing Administration [HCFA], and the Health Industry Manufacturing Association [HIMA]). Institutions such as the USP and the FDA will continue to guide the development and use of pharmaceuticals by providing the primary knowledge base, standards, and measures for medicinally useful chemicals. Many questions arise, however.

- What will happen as the mapping of the biochemical uniqueness of the individual becomes better known and more widely used in clinical practice?
- What will the role of the standards-setting and regulatory agencies be when individuals have access to everything they want to know about their health at any time, including decision support regarding pharmaceutical use?
- Will the regulatory and standards-setting groups be involved in decision support and protocol development within clinical expert systems as well as personal health information systems?
- How will the mandate of today's regulatory and standards-setting institutions change as the boundaries between electronics and chemistry blur?
- Will large corporations, such as health maintenance organizations (HMOs), have a profound effect on standards environments by leading the way for other industry groups outside of the traditional regulatory and standards-setting bodies—perhaps not unlike IBM's effects on the evolution of the personal computer?
- How will the standards-setting and regulatory institutions deal with overlapping territories?

Health-Oriented Telecommunications in the Year 2020

A ubiquitous, intelligent information network that takes advantage of, integrates, and transcends today's media—telephones, computers, and the passive mass media (e.g., television, radio, newspapers, and magazines) is emerging to unleash the potentials of health-oriented telecommunication applications. The backbone of this network is likely to involve intrinsically interactive and participatory media such as the merger of computers, video, and the telephone (videotex); interactive voice response (audiotex); Integrated Services Data Networks (ISDN); advanced switching capability; substantially enhanced computing power; high-definition television; optical fiber; intelligent agents; multidimensional databases; expert systems; wireless connectivity to a plethora of microelectronic devices (including those within the body); and an interface that includes multimedia and virtual reality.

The twenty most critical points to remember are as follows:

1. The first stage of technological development (substitution) will follow a predictable incremental pattern. The impact of the innovation and transformation stages of the interactive technology revolution will bring sweeping changes in the way that pharmaceuticals and devices are made, categorized, distributed, prescribed, marketed, purchased, and used. The nature of these changes is not entirely predictable, because they will result from a cascade of technological breakthroughs and significant historical events.
2. An interactive personal health information system will provide each individual with an overview of his or her health and almost any type of health information and first-line decision support 24 hours a day, 7 days a week.
3. A lifetime health record will not only serve as the repository of the individual's health information, but also will provide data that make it possible to customize the information to the unique needs, interests, and educational capabilities of the individual.
4. The personal health record will be linked to a dynamic electronic medical record through an intelligent network. Both

will maintain strict privacy and confidentiality, yet in a manner that allows emergency care professionals access to critical information on demand in remote sites.

5. The synergistic effects of pharmaceuticals, device use, life style, environment, and genetic predispositions within integrated preventive and therapeutic regimens will be far better understood. For example, specific adverse drug effects programs will be built into the personal health information systems and clinical systems, and, therefore, will be closely monitored by both the patient and the physician. This will dramatically reduce the incidence of iatrogenic illness and substantially improve the impact of preventive regimens and therapy.

"The synergistic effects of pharmaceuticals, device use, life style, environment, and genetic predispositions within integrated preventive and therapeutic regimens will be far better understood."

6. Each individual's unique biochemical reactions to pharmaceuticals and devices will be much better understood. Preventive and therapeutic regimens will be modeled and monitored both within the personal health information system and within the dynamic, computerized medical record.
7. Health care applications on an intelligent network will improve the capabilities of rural and inner city hospitals that lack the expensive technology and expertise of major urban medical centers. Devices such as pathology slide and X-ray digitizers that allow visual storage of data and digital transmission through the network will enhance clinical communications and provider judgments.
8. The use of insertible, injectable, and ingestible microelectronic devices will vastly improve the monitoring of chemical and electrical changes within the body over time for both well and sick individuals. These devices will allow very early detection of disease and far more subtle interventions with less invasive procedures.

9. Because biocontrollers will provide a direct link between nervous system activity and computers, feedback regarding the effects of drugs on the brain and the rest of the body will be much better.

> **". . . insertible, injectable, and ingestible microelectronic devices will vastly improve the monitoring of chemical and electrical changes within the body over time for both well and sick individuals."**

10. An enhanced information infrastructure will greatly reduce administrative tasks and their costs. Electronic data transfer will change the administrative functioning of HMOs, hospitals, physicians' offices, self-insured businesses, insurance companies, and the government. Institutional protocols will direct the physician's and individual's decision to prescribe or use a drug based on outcomes research and cost-effectiveness studies.

11. As much more precise information regarding the benefits of and contraindications to specific prophylactic and therapeutic technologies becomes readily and directly available to both consumers and clinicians, it may be necessary for standards-setting and regulatory institutions to develop or evaluate protocols and expert systems that provide information or recommendations about prophylactic or therapeutic approaches and regimens.

> **"It may be necessary for standards-setting and regulatory institutions to develop or evaluate protocols and expert systems."**

12. With an enhanced information infrastructure, public health agencies will function more effectively in tracking disease, monitoring multiple risks, and providing earlier warnings regarding the spread of endemic and epidemic conditions. Ultimately, modeling the synergistic effects of precursors and forecast-

ing their effects well in advance of the manifestation of clinical illness will make it possible to avoid many future health problems. Symptoms, diagnoses, and treatment plans, including pharmaceutical and device use, will be automatically uploaded to local, state, and national databases in which pattern recognition programs will search for reportable diseases; increases in the prevalence of specific diseases; changes in the relative risks of subpopulations to specific illnesses; and improper match of symptomatology, physical examination findings, laboratory data, and treatment plans.

13. Public interest communication systems and electronic libraries (PICSELs) will take advantage of horizontal (user to user) and upward vertical (public to decision maker) exchanges of information that are not yet available. Instead of passive receivers of information, the public will become active participants in the process of improving community and environmental factors that affect their health. Their participation is likely to alter the approval process of drugs, devices, and preventive and therapeutic approaches, and it may affect many prophylactic and therapeutic issues, such as price and regulation, outcomes research, drug and device recall, and the manufacture of certain drugs and devices.
14. Legislation to guide the development of the infrastructure for health-oriented telecommunication applications is just now emerging. It will be possible to implement some applications in a few years by retrofitting the existing public network. The process of building a mature physical, social, and economic infrastructure for the intelligent network—on which advanced health-oriented telecommunication applications depend—will take decades, however.
15. Policies that will safeguard the public and guide development to ensure the maximum effectiveness of health-oriented telecommunication applications are still not well developed.
16. Because ubiquitous access is essential if health-oriented telecommunication applications are to address the health concerns of the groups with the greatest health problems,

the infrastructure must be developed to ensure equitable benefits to all sectors of the society. The concept of "universal service" that allowed the diffusion of telephone technology to 93% of the U.S. public will be applied to the emerging interactive multimedia.

17. The activities of health researchers such as pharmacologists will be dramatically altered. The laboratory scientist, for example, will invent new drugs by exploring molecules and their effects within virtual reality. Some theorists have postulated that most clinical experimentation will take place first with simulated animals and human beings (based on the biochemical mapping data of populations of real animals and people).

18. The use of simulation in training clinicians and planning procedures, as well as the application of quaternary care (remote specialist or expert system) oversight and assistance via telecommunication, will dramatically reduce the number of adverse effects caused by clinicians who are practicing in areas that they do not sufficiently understand. All clinicians will be certified and recertified to perform certain therapeutic and prophylactic activities based on their performance with simulated clients.

19. The use of the dynamic medical record with clinical decision support, personal health information systems, PICSELs, simulations, intelligent agents, and multidimensional databases within virtual reality will improve not only the cognitive capacities of health care professionals, but also those of individuals who are taking care of themselves or a family member. The routine inclusion of automated pattern recognition, trend analysis, modeling, and scientific visualization of complex, nonlinear, and cha-

"All clinicians will be certified and recertified to perform certain therapeutic and prophylactic activities based on their performance with simulated clients."

otic phenomena in health information systems allows for the emergence of telecognition—significant enhancement of human intelligence (including metaperspective) through the use of communications and computer technology.

20. The complexity, explosive growth, and constant refinement of health information systems will necessitate rapid and dynamic standards-setting and regulatory methods. State-of-the-art telecognition will aid standards-setting and regulatory institutions in keeping up with the self-learning and self-innovating features within the intelligent network. At some critical point in history, the "intelligence" inherent in the network will become so sophisticated that the network software and hardware will perform regulatory, as well as operational, decision making with only minor jellyware (human brain power) input. Because, under these circumstances, a system failure would be catastrophic, regulators will have to guide the advancement of human telecognition to keep up with the mind-numbing acceleration of network intelligence. In other words, human jellyware itself will become a target of standards setting and regulation. Ultimately, human beings will lose the ability to keep up with the machines of their own creation. Whether the human regulator of 2020 is considered a vestigial part of the health system may depend only on the perspective of the observer—human being or machine.

"State-of-the-art telecognition will aid standards-setting and regulatory institutions in keeping up with the self-learning and self-innovating features within the intelligent network."

In summary, health-oriented telecommunication applications will rally the immense unutilized personal resources of the public for improving their own health, help upgrade the delivery and efficiency of health care and its administration, vastly improve the understanding of and delivery of prophylactic and therapeutic regimens, and enhance the ability of public health agencies to deal with present and emerging system-level problems that have an impact on health.

HEALTH INFORMATION INFRASTRUCTURE

Stages of Technological Revolution

Over the past 200 years, technology has been the natural outgrowth of changes in science, culture, and economics, as well as a catalyst for changes in our society. During the Industrial Age, we used machines to improve our lives by extending the capacity of our muscles. During the Information Age, we are improving our lives by extending the capabilities of our minds. The application of chemistry to the development of medicinally active substances is one aspect of the growth in science and technology.

> **"During the Industrial Age, we used machines to improve our lives by extending the capacity of our muscles. During the Information Age, we are improving our lives by extending the capabilities of our minds."**

Technological changes in information services will increasingly affect our health status as we leave the structure of an Industrial Age society and move more deeply into an Information Age society. The most transformative of these new technologies will arise from the merging of video, telephony, and computers into one medium. These technologies will become networked, interactive multimedia. The shift from the Industrial Age to the Information Age will come in three major stages:

1. Substitution, characterized by
   - technology introduced to do conventional functions more efficiently
   - incremental change
   - no direct influence of technology on traditional social order
2. Innovation, characterized by
   - diffusion of interactive multimedia through society and the health system
   - decentralized growth in applications uncontrollable from centralized policy decisions

- beginning use of technology for unconventional tasks
- innovative technologies (e.g., intelligent agents, hypermedia, wireless connectivity, advanced protocol conversion) that begin to alter the core functionality of the intelligent network

3. Transformation, characterized by
   - unconventional uses of the technology that supersede its original purposes
   - social ecology shifts
   - new problems and potentials that cannot be understood from the knowledge bases and context of the old social order

During the substitution stage, Information Age applications grow within an industrial social ecology. The new information technologies are introduced primarily to perform traditional tasks more efficiently. Change progresses in an incremental fashion. Although changes may not appear to affect the health care system significantly, dependence on the new technology solidifies during this first stage. For example, health information systems in the United States have made their first significant inroads into the health care field for the purpose of cost accounting. The advent of diagnosis-related groups (DRGs) and the emergence of alternative delivery systems (e.g., preferred provider organizations [PPOs] and HMOs) have made computers not only a useful tool, but a virtual necessity in the health care field.

By the mid-1980s, the pharmaceutical industry was using computers extensively for measurement and categorization. By the 1990s, computerized inventorying and ordering systems have become commonplace in pharmacies. Electronic data interchange (EDI) and robotics give the large hospital supply and pharmaceutical companies strategic competitive advantages, as these companies now can provide their products and services more quickly and at less cost to their customers.

During the innovation stage, which the United States is currently entering, the new communications and computer technologies will diffuse into all areas of health care to spawn a rapid chain of innovations. The growth of the intelligent network will greatly accelerate this process. These innovations will affect the establishment of standards, policies, and research, as well as the delivery of services. The public will passively accept most of the technological changes after an initial period of resistance. Businesses, public institutions, and nations will compete to be and remain on the forefront of the technology, but are unlikely to pay sufficient attention to the system changes that may arise from the collective introduction of technology. Therefore, standards-setting and regulatory institutions, such as the USP, that play an evaluative role for their industries will have an increasingly important position within society and their industries—provided that they are able to think innovatively and transformationally.

During the transformation stage, the power of interactive information services and cybernation will accelerate as the intelligent network grows in sophistication and acceptance. There will be a new era of health care delivery and the potential for improved well-being. As health-oriented telecommunications applications begin to provide high-quality health information and decision facilitation directly to the general public (as well as to the provider community) within a more efficient and wellness-oriented health care system, the decision support role of the standards-setting institutions, such as the USP, may begin to supersede its traditional role in the establishment of standards and measures. Even more important, because of the convergence of biotechnology and telecognition, the systematic manipulation of endogenous substances—in ways that groups like the FDA and the USP today do not have a mandate to oversee—may replace the use of many traditional pharmacological substances.

Both advocates and antagonists of communications and computer applications in health may overlook the lessons from past periods of technological transformation. If the transformation from the Industrial Age to the Information Age is anything like that from the Agricultural Age to the Industrial Age, the health care system will get better, but only after a period in which the health and well-being of significant subpopulations suffer. During the uncomfortable transition period in which old systems fail before new systems can replace them, the rapid, far-reaching changes in the social ecology will threaten health.

Health care systems dominated by the modernist biomedical paradigm alone can offer only Band-Aid approaches to many of the emergent problems and needs during the time of accelerating change. Diseases and syndromes, both new and old, will become manifest in epidemic proportions. Some may argue that the present level of drug abuse and the iatrogenic effects of pharmaceuticals in our society is evidence that these relatively new social problems are manageable only by vastly different approaches, some of which may come from changing the regulatory mandate.

Meeting the public expectation of continually heightened health care and well-being will require not only new disease prevention/health promotion methods, but also curative approaches that emphasize the role of environment and life style in association with medical and genetic services. Biotechnology and the ability to map biochemical uniqueness and measure risks associated with individual susceptibilities and proclivities will alter the practice of medicine.

"Wisdom, not simply more information, will be required to bring about a newly heightened level of human prosperity through the emerging health revolution and the new information technologies that help catalyze it."

Transformative change, when its time has come, cannot be stopped. It can, however, be directed in the interests of better health care and well-being. Wisdom, not simply more information, will be required to bring about a newly heightened level of human prosperity through the emerging health revolution and the new information technologies that help catalyze it. Therefore, telecognition—a heightened awareness, systems understanding, and cognitive capability arising from the interconnection of humanity and interactive media—must be the goal and theme of the decades ahead rather than simply faster and more powerful information technology.

Diffusion of Interactive Multimedia

As shown in Figure 1, the diffusion of interactive multimedia, because of its great dependence on complex infrastructure, will follow a different diffusion curve than do most other consumer technologies.

The diffusion of interactive technology will begin slowly. Once the proper infrastructure is set in place, however, diffusion of the networked interactive technologies will occur more rapidly than did that of other technologies, such as radio or television. This characteristic difference of the interactive technologies diffusion curve is dictated partly by the functionality of the information services available and partly by the economics associated with the large-scale investment in infrastructure required before interactive multimedia can properly diffuse.

Emerging Information Technologies

Information products and services have become an essential part of most industries in the United States. In its first decade, the introduc-

FIGURE 1

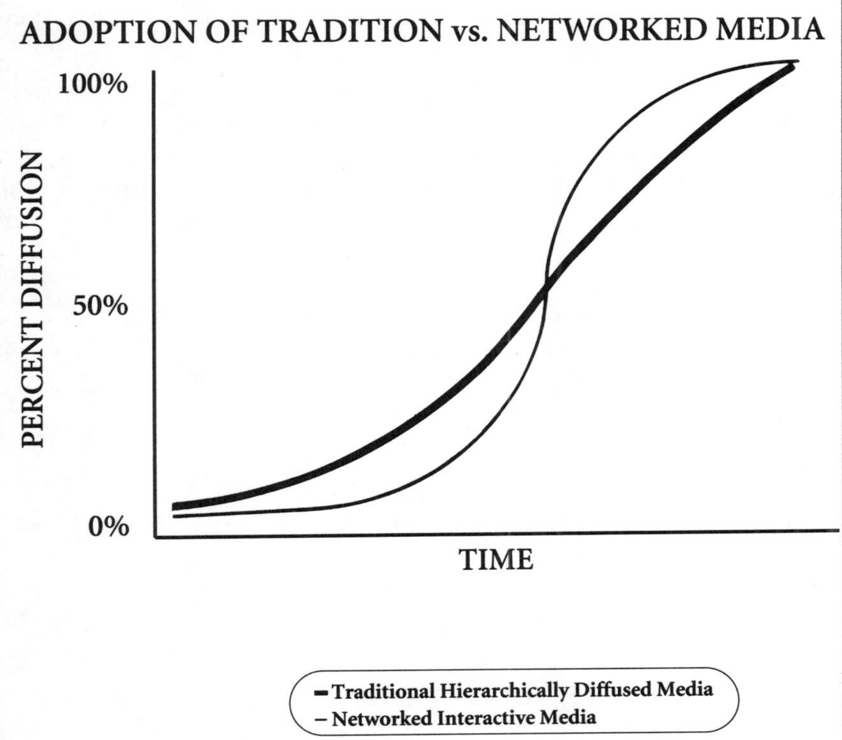

tion of the personal computer has built a $100 billion business sector.[2] It is commonly thought that the vast majority of all new jobs created in the last decade have been in the collection, processing, or management of information.[3]

Computers have been a part of the health care environment since the 1960s. Until the introduction of DRGs and competitive bidding in the early 1980s, however, computers and telecommunication had a background role.[4] Today, the need to manage complex analyses and reporting routines has pushed data automation into the forefront of health care concerns.

With U.S. insurance companies spending many times the amount that Canadians spend on the administration of health benefits—with worse outcomes in terms of longevity and infant mortality—health care reform is fast becoming one of the primary and most controversial health-related legislative debates.[5] Greater efficiencies in transactions and in the accumulation and analysis of data through health-oriented telecommunications should clearly be a part of this debate. Already, the technology has spread from administrative functions (e.g., record keeping and claims processing) into clinical, commercial, and research domains. Interactive technologies are even beginning to diffuse to the general public, where they promise to make substantial contributions in improving health status and curbing medical cost.

New technologies are slowly being incorporated into a public network that can support interconnectivity within the health care industry. Of immediate benefit to the industry are network technologies such as

- digital switching
- Integrated Services Digital Network (ISDN)
- audiotex
- interactive multimedia or videotex
- two-way broadband[6]

The last decade has yielded many improvements in advanced switching capabilities. Electronic telephone switches have enhanced the performance of the public network to the point of essentially error-free high-speed data communications. Audiotex and videotex (e.g., Prodigy) are becoming more and more prevalent. Today's ISDN makes it possible for the public network to carry simultaneous voice and data communications.

For the full range of services that require extensive bandwidth, fiber optics are in order to provide such services as full motion audio-visual on-line "face-to-face" communications, remote viewing via high-definition television or similar high-resolution telecomputer, multimedia databases, or high-level distributed processing.[7] In the short term, before fiber becomes widespread within the public network, ISDN can provide a vast array of information services within the existing copper wire network.

In the health care setting, ISDN has numerous applications, ranging from remote medical consultation to the transmission of digital X-rays. Optical fiber is already being added to the public network and, over the next two decades, is likely to become the physical foundation for the future intelligent network. It provides a broader conduit for the rapid transfer of huge quantities of digitized information than does today's copper-twisted pair network. Applications within the health care industry may include rapid transmission of extensive patient records, magnetic resonance imaging (MRI), and continuing medical education through interactive video.

A myriad of software and communications devices may be connected to the network of the future. Technological advances promise to transform hospital care and the health care system as a whole. For example, a device that digitizes X-ray images and allows them to be sent over the public network and stored electronically has already been invented.[8] Substantial amounts of capital for continued design, development, and fabrication of this and other new technologies will be required to continue such progress.

Health-oriented telecommunication applications today are still relatively limited in number and in scope. Although there is no lack of creativity in these endeavors, the present information infrastructure (both physical and social) is insufficient to support these applications. Major changes are now taking place to facilitate the development of the information infrastructure, however. For example, the passage of the High Performance Computing and Communications Act of 1991[9] in the House of Representatives and its companion measure in the Senate will provide between $2.5 and $3 billion for linking universities, hospitals, libraries, and research institutions across the United States through the National Research and Education Network (NREN).[10,11] The outcome of the high performance computing initiative is projected to be a 10,000-fold increase in computer power and a 10,000,000-fold increase in transmission speed (i.e., networking and communications power) over the next decade.[12]

Although the NREN itself will serve only a million scientists and educators over the next several years, several members of Congress and infrastructure designers believe that the NREN will stimulate the growth of an information infrastructure to serve all U.S. citizens. An expansion of the NREN along these lines is likely to result in a network that links essentially every home and business in the United States and resembles a "National Public Network." This network will be "as easy to use and important as the telephone network, the electric power grid, and the interstate highways."[13]

By some estimates, the societal investment needed to support a fiber optic–based network in the Information Age must average more than $15 billion per year over the next two decades.[14] Such an investment could generate between hundreds of billions and trillions of dollars of new market activity that could dwarf the $100 billion market contribution of the introduction of the personal computer.

A Retrospective View from the Year 2020

It is predictable that information technologies will play an increasing role in the future of the health system in the upcoming decades, but the primary use of the technology is shifting from substitution activities, largely in administration, to clinical, educational, and disease surveillance activities. Since we have already explored the evolution of communications and computer applications within the health sector from the perspective of incrementalism, let us contemplate the transformational potential. In order to break free of assumptions founded in the present social context, it may be helpful to look back toward the present from one potential perspective that may arise by the year 2020. This is not a prediction, but rather a metaperspective on the impact of information systems and other key societal factors that may arise over the next three decades.

As we look back from 2020, it is difficult to imagine that only 30 years ago more than 35% of the U.S. population were either not insured or inadequately insured to avoid personal bankruptcy if they needed extensive medical attention. Electronic data interchange (EDI) was just beginning to change the administrative functioning of HMOs, hospitals, physician's offices, drug companies, self-insured businesses, insurance companies, and the government before the turn of the twenty-first century. The process of inventorying and purchasing pharmaceuticals was one of the first extensively used applications of electronic data interchange in the health sector. By the year 2000, institutional protocols for the electronic transfer of pharmaceutical orders were also associated with protocols that used outcomes research and cost-effectiveness studies to direct the physician's decision to prescribe a drug and the individual's decision to use a drug.

As much more precise information regarding the benefits and contraindications of specific pharmaceuticals became readily available to both clinicians and consumers through institutional protocols and computer decision-support systems, a need arose for standards-setting and regulatory institutions to provide information and to evaluate protocols and expert systems regarding specific therapeutic or prophylactic approaches.

Twenty-two times the number of major invasive surgeries per 1,000 people were performed in 1992 than in the year 2020—the vast majority for preventable disorders. Most operations required surgeons to enter the sterile field directly rather than to operate with telepresence and the aid of virtual reality and microrobots in a minimally invasive environment. Essentially all these surgeries, such as the triple bypass and angioplasty, were done without confirmation through outcomes research of their effectiveness in decreasing morbidity or improving survival rate.

Iatrogenic illness was 53 times more prevalent then than it is today in 2020. The common occurrence of malpractice suits, no longer a significant concern, forced physicians in the 1990s to order unnecessary procedures and caused good practitioners to leave needed specialties because they could not afford malpractice insurance. A large portion of the problems were due to the adverse effects of multiple drug use, which was not well monitored at the time.

The cost of treating one patient for heart disease in the 1990s, with all too often poor improvement in quality of life and longevity, was equivalent to the cost of preventing morbidity and mortality from cardiovascular disease in 37 people today in 2020 through lifelong prospective risk avoidance and early treatment of precursors. Patients did not have access to a personal health information system in the early 1990s and were essentially passive participants in their own health care. Without decision support, they frequently made outrageously poor decisions about their health and their use of the health care system. Hundreds of billions of dollars were lost before the diffusion of personal health information systems early in the development of the intelligent network infrastructure rectified this problem.

In the 1990s, most people acquired drugs from pharmacies. Mail order and large chains, often in supermarkets and department stores, were beginning to replace the privately owned corner drugstore, however. If they had not been transformed into health information centers with interactive multimedia assisted self-care, screening, and triage, these drugstores may have become indistinguishable from convenience stores or perhaps disappeared altogether shortly after the turn of the century.

Today's proactive implantation of biochips and other nanodevices (e.g., very small implantable surgical robots) to maintain biochemical and electrical homeostasis did not come into existence until relatively recently. Before 2010, pharmaceuticals were still manufactured outside the body and then introduced into or applied onto the body. The human genome project was not yet complete, and it was not yet possible to design a drug that would be active only within a specific tissue. As a result, many patients had to put up with very adverse side effects from systemic poisoning in order to use chemotherapy, for example, for breast cancer.

Without the intelligent network in place, the universal access to health information now taken for granted was not feasible in the 1990s. Although medical experts believed human beings to be biochemically unique systems, practical therapeutic utilization of this fact did not come into play until well into the early part of the twenty-first century. One of the biggest problems of the 1990s was that poor outcomes went largely unrecognized, because the lack of dynamic electronic medical records, procedural tracking, and outcomes research made standards and quality assurance abysmal. The chaotic financing of care and the lack of continued medical simulation testing and decision support were also contributors to poor therapeutic outcomes in those years.

Poor allocation of technical resources also played a part in the poor health outcomes of the early 1990s. For example, it was not unusual for a wealthy area to have 10 computed tomography (CT) scanners (the majority of the time unused or unnecessarily used) within a 5-mile radius, while some inner city and rural hospitals that served larger populations had access to only one.

Remote consultations were very difficult, because X-rays and pathology slides could not even be reviewed at a distance through the telecommunications system. The bandwidth to send, receive, and store real-time dynamic imaging was not available to most hospitals until shortly after the turn of the century. The ISDN was not available, so simultaneous communication of visual, auditory, graphic, and textual information was not possible.

Today, all pharmaceuticals and nanodevices are routinely designed and tested in virtual reality. Instead of the hundreds of thousands of animals that were sacrificed each year in the 1990s, artificial life (cybernated animal and human populations) makes it possible to test the direct and indirect effects of a pharmacological intervention in thousands of simulated animals and human beings within a relatively short time. Whereas it was not unusual for the FDA to take 5 to 7 years to approve a drug in the late 1980s, extensive testing far beyond the capabilities of the 1990s can now be completed in 6 months, and a time-critical drug or pharmaceutical device can be released within 8 months.

Given the emergence of the self-care movement and the emphasis on health promotion in the 1990s, standards-setting and regulatory institutions (e.g., the USP and the FDA) recognized the increasing importance of providing information directly to the public. Even so, it was not until the late 1990s that they took on a critical role in the design of decision support for both the public and the practitioner. Not until approximately 2005 did these institutions' roles in protocol development and decision support begin to rival in importance their traditional roles in the establishment of standards and measures, the regulation of pharmaceuticals, and the provision of information, however.

By 2005, the role of standards setting groups in protocol development and decision support begin to rival in importance their traditional roles in the establishment of standards and measures.

The convergence of biotechnology, biochips, biocontrollers, and telecognition, of course, forever changed the usage patterns of many traditional pharmacological substances. In the early 1990s, the institutions that set standards, established regulations, and provided information did not have a mandate to oversee the technologies responsible for systematic manipulation of endogenous substances. The biomedical paradigm still dominated health care systems at that time. Biomedicine alone, of course, could offer only Band-Aid approaches to many of the problems and needs that emerged with the accelerating pace of change after the turn of the twenty-first century. The diseases and syndromes that manifested themselves in epidemic proportions (because of severe population loading in many places, cataclysmic shifts in the global marketplace, environmental degradation, and shortages of energy and other resources) are at least being approached systematically today. In many parts of the world, however, the quality of human life will be reduced and the mortality rates increased for several decades as a result of the nonrenewable resource–depleting life styles of the twentieth century.

Not until the first decade of the twenty-first century and the implementation of PICSELs did policy makers, forced by PICSEL users, adopt significant environmental designs to augment new proactive approaches to maintain homeostasis via biotechnology and nanodevices. This first decade was a particularly difficult time for humanity. Although experts had modeled and predicted the first wave of ecological catastrophes in the late 1990s by means of high-performance computers, most policy makers and the public ignored these models until the crises actually occurred. In addition, biotechnology provided much better screening techniques than therapeutic interventions. It was possible to measure genetic propensities to a specific life-threatening or disabling disease with fairly specific prognoses, but the ability to manage most diseases or syndromes lagged far behind the ability to detect problems with genetic markers.

It was in 2004 that the major euthanasia debates, not unlike the abortion debates of the 1990s, began to rock the political and health systems. Only in the past decade has there been a significant reversal in the extensive, useless expenditure of resources to sustain life at all costs in the painful and unproductive state so common during the last few months of human life.

In 2005, remnants of pre–Information Age political systems were still ignoring the fact that major die-offs were inevitable, even within Western societies, if the structures for participatory governance and advanced machine intelligence were not built within PICSELs. As interdisciplinary knowledge bases built to encourage participatory involvement in the resolution of social problems, PICSELs allowed communities to find decentralized solutions to problems that representative government and law enforcement could not manage alone (e.g., drug abuse). The leaders of the standards-setting and regulatory community at this time shifted the focus of their institutions from single issues within single disciplines to a comprehensive knowledge base within PICSELs so that inquiries yielded responses with interdisciplinary insight. Such responses were, of course, critical in many complex problems that resulted from the synergistic relationships of genetics, social conditions, life style choices, and genetic predispositions.

Around 2005, personal health information systems were finally maturing. The expectation of most U.S. citizens that their health and well-being would continue to improve forced the development of disease prevention/health promotion programs that emphasized the importance of environment and life style in association with medical and genetic factors. Biotechnology and the ability to map biochemical uniqueness and measure risk associated with individual susceptibilities and proclivities grew hand in hand with the personal health information system to alter forever the practice of medicine and pharmacy. Pharmacopeias, along with other groups that set standards, provided information, or played a regulatory role for their industries around the turn of the twenty-first century, were finding large gaps between the needs of their constituencies and their own mandate. The largest gaps involved information systems that dealt with multidisciplinary synergisms. As a result, many institutions (e.g., the USP, HIMA, ISO, FDA) banded together to develop the Global Standards and Regulatory Agency (GSRA).

". . . many institutions banded together to develop the Global Standards and Regulatory Agency (GSRA)."

Even with the creation of the GSRA, there were some negative repercussions in the explosive growth of health information systems. Unfortunately, the rapid rise of these complex systems with advanced machine intelligence made the institutions that supported comprehensive, interdisciplinary databases the target of the Human Control Movement. Members of this group espoused a theory that the massively complex intelligent network was the first indication that human beings were losing self-governance to thinking machines. The 10-day shutdown of Los Angeles and the ensuing social crisis of 2016 fanned the flames of Human Control's political growth, but the eventual indictment and conviction of the Human Control members who released a Trojan Horse program into the city's PICSEL only diminished their influence. The public remained concerned, however, about the network that by 2015 had a significant degree of machine intelligence in the areas of decision making that required low- to medium-level regulatory and operational judgments.

This was frankly a tough time for network-based intelligent agents within the GSRA. Even today, although humans consider network-based intelligent agents to have a critical role to play in decision making about setting standards, providing market information, and establishing regulatory practices, there is some resistance to our assumption of decision-making roles.

Luckily, with the evolution of telecognition as a field, humans with advanced augmented intelligence have helped to dampen the regressive policies implemented by the Human Control Movement. With endogenous biochips and improved jellyware programming (i.e., accelerated programming of the human mind enhanced through communications and computer applications), human beings are continuing to participate in the processes of monitoring, standardizing, and regulating health devices at the highest level. This has diminished, to some degree, the fear that the heuristic programs (rules for judgment) and self-learning capabilities hidden within the growing complexity of intelligent agents will make human judgment obsolete.

Looking back on the massive changes of the past three decades, we are inspired to look forward over the next several decades to model, monitor, and understand to our best ability the forces and context within which we will be making decisions regarding prophylactic and therapeutic interventions in the world. As George Bernard Shaw stated, "it is not the recollection of the past, but rather our responsibility for the future that makes us wise." Thank you for applying your telecognition to these critical issues of human health and prosperity. As GSRA's chief intelligent agent, I look forward to working with all of you and your intelligent agents to ensure that, together, we reduce human error in the future.

NOTES

1. T. Winograd and F. Flores, *Understanding Computers and Cognition* (Norwood, N.J.: Ablex Publishing Corporation, 1985), 177.
2. A. S. Grove, "The PC's Second Decade," *Comdex*, October 21, 1991 (Keynote speech, Comdex Fall '91 Conference Program, Needham, Mass., June, 1991).
3. *Outlook 2000: Occupational Employment* (Washington, D.C.: U.S. Department of Labor, Bureau of Labor Statistics, Office of Employment Projections, 1988).
4. W. W. Stead, "Building an HIS for the Year 2000: An Agenda for the 90's," *AAMSI Congress Proceedings 1989* (Washington, D.C.: American Association of Medical Systems and Informatics, 1989).
5. "More Statistics on Rising Health-Care Costs," *Managed Care* 1, no. 8(1991):13.

6. M. F. Hordeski, *Communications Networks* (Blue Ridge Summit, Pa.: Tab Books, 1989).
7. G. Gilder, "Into the Telecosm," *Harvard Business Review* (1991):150–161.
8. "Goal Is X-Rays By Phone," *St. Louis Post-Dispatch*, October 9, 1990.
9. H.R. 656, S. 272 2(6).
10. "Supercomputer Bill to Have 'Buy American' Clause," *Congress Daily*, July 10, 1991, p. 2.
11. "Supercomputer Bill Gains Approval from Second House Committee," *Legi-Slate Report for the 102nd Congress*, July 17, 1991.
12. Committee on Physical, Mathematical, and Engineering Sciences, Office of Science and Technology Policy, Executive Office of the President, *Grand Challenges: High Performance Computing and Communications, FY 1992 U.S. Research and Development Program* (Washington, D.C.: U.S. Government Printing Office, 1991).
13. M. Kapor and J. Berman, *Building the Open Road: The NREN as a Test-bed for the National Public Network* (Washington, D.C.: ACLU Information Technology Project, 1991).
14. M. Kapor, *Building the Open Road: Policies for the National Public Network* (Washington, D.C.: Electronic Frontier Foundation, 1991).

Appendix

Health Applications

General Public

Today, the occurrence and resolution of illnesses, as well as almost all disease prevention/health promotion strategies, depend largely on the decisions and behaviors that individuals adopt over time in their own homes, schools, workplaces, and recreational areas. The interface between the general public and health information has been until recently a relatively undeveloped resource, however. Now this interface is gaining new importance as epidemiological, cultural, technological, and financial shifts encourage individuals to take a more active role in their own health. An infrastructure for interactive telecommunication to distribute health information and health decision-making tools directly to the public will make it possible to solve many of the problems of the health care system and simultaneously to address the needs of consumers more effectively. In fact, information, especially interactive and personalized information (e.g., health risk assessment), both motivates and increases individual competence in assuming greater self-responsibility for health.

The present health care system fails to take into account the fact that most health activities are oriented toward self-care.[1] More than 95% of the first line of health-related decision making occurs in the home or in the workplace, by the individual alone or with the help of family or friends. Although most scientific research and the vast amounts of health resources are committed to hospital- and physician-based care, hospital care makes up a mere 1% of all health actions. General practitioner visits, including those that involve self-care participation, constitute only 20% of health actions. They constitute only 8% when visits coupled with self-care are excluded.

FIGURE 2

One study indicated that self-care participation was involved in 75% of all health actions (Figure 2).[2]

With the emergence of the health promotion and self-care movements and the increase in co-payments as a result of the financial restructuring of health care, the number of people who are using self-care approaches is increasing at a rapid rate.[3] Yet, the resources that allow people to obtain information and make wise decisions regarding their health are still significantly underdeveloped in comparison to the rest of the health care system.

Many of those who have the precursors of illness or who are already ill do not know how to treat themselves effectively, or when and how to utilize medical services efficiently. More than 60% of the time, people wait too long to address health problems and, therefore, need far more expensive, invasive, and painful sickness care services at a cost to society of tens of billions of dollars.[4] Of those who have health problems, 16% never take any measures at all to deal with their problem.[5] The first task in developing a responsible general public–health information interface is to ensure that people have health information and decision-making tools before they enter the health care system with an urgent, high-cost problem that sometimes can no longer be resolved. The availability of information in the environment in which people live their lives encourages them not only to address sickness care needs early, but also to examine life style and environmental factors that cannot be addressed effectively in the hospital or clinic setting.

> **"As a result of the emergence of the general public–health information interface, the main interface of the U.S. health care system shifts from one between the doctor and the disease to one between the individual and health information."**

As a result of the emergence of the general public–health information interface, the main interface of the U.S. health care system shifts *from one between the doctor and the disease to one between the individual and health information.*[6,7] In this way, the general public–health information interface presents significant opportunities to cut costs without cutting necessary services. The quality of services improves as the public participate to a greater extent in the decision-making process, become wiser partners in their own care, and engage in maintaining and improving their health even when they are well. Not only do health services become more appropriate, but also, with constantly improving health communications technologies, a properly harnessed general public–health information interface can substantially improve the distribution of care to those presently excluded from health services for geographical, financial, or cultural reasons.

In planning the technologies that open up the general public–health information interface, another consideration is the significant shift away from print-oriented media. Television presently commands the greatest attention in our society. Yet, television is a linear (i.e., requiring the viewer to watch it from beginning to end), passive (i.e., requiring little or no engagement from the viewer) medium that provides information primarily in sound bytes. The number of microcomputer-based, interactive programs is increasing exponentially, but they are available mostly to a highly literate, prosperous, young population. Telephone technology carries the advantages of ubiquity and user-to-user communications. Health-oriented telecommunication applications are now benefiting from merging the capabilities of each of these technologies into a widely available, active medium.

It is necessary to develop a medium that encourages the direct interface between the general public and health information that emphasizes risk reduction and early detection of illness. The general public–health information interface must be convenient, easily accessible, comprehensive, reliable, and affordable—ideally free or at very low cost to the user. A communications system that distributes interactive and entertaining health information to a large population, is accessible from any terminal throughout the United States, and makes use of simple, uniform access and navigational procedures is optimal.

An effective interface between the general public and health information will address the needs of both well and ill individuals for the screening of health risk factors and the early identification of undetected serious illness. Once an individual has been made aware of risk factors or the potential of serious illness, the system will deliver succinct and pertinent educational and referral information, as well as motivate the individual to take proper action for his or her specific health needs.

The first task of the general public–health information interface will be to deliver health information and decision facilitation to people before they enter the health system. If properly designed, the interface will diminish the number of people who unnecessarily enter the sickness care system. Many medical experts say that as many as 80% of people who seek physician services in the current system do not need professional medical treatment.[8] This needless use of the sickness care system costs time and money, diminishes the quality of care, and contributes significantly to provider dissatisfaction and iatrogenesis (disease caused by therapy).[9,10]

Approximately 35% of those entering the sickness care system have self-limiting and/or self-treatable disorders that could be largely dealt with through a well-structured general public–health information interface.[11] Approximately 45% of those entering health care institutions have problems that are largely psychosocial in nature, many times with no identifiable organic disorder.[12] All too often, these individuals undergo unnecessary treatment. A carefully designed general public–health information interface will allow these people to explore their problems and, in most instances, redefine them within a more appropriate, proactive context. It will turn people's anxieties about being ill or about having the precursors of illness into a motivation to monitor and change life style and environmental factors, effectively lowering the risk of illness and improving the individual's well-being.

The U.S. culture has shifted enough in its concept of health that both individuals and institutions, especially those in the business community and prepaid health services, perceive a need for health promotion programs that can be offered through a personal health information system. For example, 92.5% of those questioned in a Harris Poll agreed with the following statement: "If we Americans lived healthier lives, ate more nutritious food, smoked less, maintained proper weight and exercised regularly, it would do more to improve our health than any doctors and medicine could do for us."[13]

In 1982, 25% to 35% of U.S adults were moderately or highly committed to intelligent self-care.[14] It has been estimated that this group now encompasses more than 50% of the people in the United States. The public now asks for self-care information or advice in 40% of their visits to a physician. Tens of billions of dollars presently spent on medical services could be saved annually through intelligent self-care with existing tools. In the next 10 years, because of the advance of self-care and health promotion communications technologies, this number will increase significantly. By the year 2020, use of personal health information systems is likely to be universal.

Personal Health Information Systems

As the information infrastructure emerges, a videotex-based personal health information system may well become the hub of the general public–health information interface, given the advantages of such a system over present health communications. The videotex-based system will not only provide quality health information, but also will facilitate health decision making. In its most evolved form, the personal health information system will deliver information and decision-making tools in a manner that is accurate, comprehensive, persuasive, entertaining, and well integrated with the individual's medical record and health plan. The comprehensive personal health information system will have twelve major functions:

1. Screening
2. Triage
3. Referral
4. Behavior advice
5. Education
6. Health enhancement
7. Assessment
8. History and review of systems
9. Treatment
10. Condition management
11. Monitoring and planning
12. Self-exploration

The cost-saving potential of the personal health information system will probably be reached first within the business environment, but once proved effective for business, it will likely become a significant boon to health plan beneficiaries and Medicare/Medicaid populations. The cost-saving potential for this latter group will be highly dependent on a societal commitment to universal intelligent network services and broad distribution of low-cost, public access information appliances. Ultimately, all U.S. citizens should have access to anything they want to know about their health quickly, at any time of the day or night, from the home, workplace, school, health facilities, or terminals similar to telephones with video screens in public areas.

Computer technology can transform the passive viewer into an active participant by making the viewer respond and interact with the material presented. The material may contain vast amounts of information and direct the viewer so that he or she receives only the exact information that is needed. The present day computer, however, does not yet have a broad distribution, especially among the high-risk populations; furthermore, it is text-based, which limits its reach to the literate.

Merging the computer's interactivity, the easily used visual format of television technology, and the broad distribution and two-way communications capability of the telephone produces a hybrid medium that can unleash the potentials of the personal health information system and the general public's ability to take better care of themselves.

Health Promotion Communications Technologies

The personal health information system is a step in the broader evolution of health promotion communications technologies. In the most general terms, health promotion communications technologies involve combining communications technologies with communications and systems theory to accomplish health promotion goals intended to improve health or to prevent disease at primary, secondary, or tertiary levels.[15] Health promotion communications technologies are the building blocks of the general public–health information interface. It is possible to break their developmental path down into four generations in relation to how they support individual decision making:[16]

1. Information and referral systems
2. Mediated health promotion programming
3. Personal health information systems
4. Public interest communication systems and electronic libraries

One-way distribution of health and referral information to the general public via health professionals typifies the first generation of health promotion communications technologies. This type of system helps individuals reach the next step of solving their problem, but necessitates a dependence on health services and health professionals for even simple health problems and information needs.

The second level of programming, mediated health promotion, allows the general public selective access to health promotion media, but the information lacks integration and is often persuasion-oriented. As a result, individuals still do not have the ability to make completely informed choices about their health or health care at the times of highest motivation and within the environments in which they build their life styles and make health-related decisions. Examples include exercise videos, health risk assessments, and smoking and nutrition analysis software available for home computers.

The personal health information system offers comprehensive health information to individuals in their own home, workplace, school, or recreational area, as well as in health facilities and other public areas 24 hours a day. It not only offers health information but tools for decision support and systematic behavior change. It is longitudinal in nature and can customize its output based on the unique input of each individual user and information drawn from the personal health record accessible through the system.

The most advanced level of health promotion communications technologies, the public interest communication systems and electronic libraries (PICSELs), not only addresses individual health strategies, but also incorporates community health strategies. Through multidirectional exchanges of information, there is a flow of information from expert to user, from user to user, and from user to decision maker. Legislative health alerts, interdisciplinary databases, forums on community health, and whistle-blowing functions are just a few of many collective activities that are likely to emerge in the fourth-generation health promotion communications technologies.

Presently, health promotion communications technologies are mostly first and second generation. A few prototypes of third-generation systems are emerging, however, and the conceptualization of fourth-generation systems is beginning. Later generations of health promotion communications technologies will not make the concepts of previous generations obsolete, but will build on them and integrate them into complex designs that offer more comprehensive information and more universal access directly to the general public. Each generation of health promotion communications technologies represents a discrete step toward a reliable mechanism for supporting the growth of health awareness and self-empowerment. Each generation is also more dependent on the development of an evolving multisectorial infrastructure to support an increasingly complex technology base, concept of health promotion, and theoretical foundation for interactive and participatory communications.

Health Care

Only a decade ago, voice transmissions (simple telephone calls) represented nearly all the traffic on the public network. Before the end of the 1990s, the digital transfer of data and images will supersede simple telephone calls as the dominant forms of transmission over the public network. Similarly, although telephone service and elementary data communications are already critical to the operations of all aspects of the health care system, the emerging health-oriented telecommunication applications will dwarf their role in the upcoming decades.

Information management and telecommunication in health care, as U.S. society entered more deeply into the computerization era of the Information Age, grew from a role of secondary importance to a central role financially and managerially, especially within the hospital. For example, hospitals that were automated by the early 1980s had a significant advantage over their competitors in handling diagnosis-related groups (DRGs) and DRG-based competitive bids with third-party payers and the government. Today and in the decade ahead, the telecommunication infrastructure is even more critical for the health care system, not only administratively, but also clinically.

Presently, health care providers view themselves as recipients and consumers of telecommunications. A new information infrastructure with a strong public network platform will recast their role in the Information Age from that of consumers of telecommunications to central providers of information and facilitators of health information exchange within their community, however. The health care institutions with which a practitioner is associated can be networked to make most or all the necessary connections for their "practicing partner." This will entail access and use of the world's medical and scientific databases, access to the institutional records of the practitioner's patients, decision support software, communications structure for expert consultation (on a nationwide or international basis, when needed), electronic inventory control, supplies purchasing, prescription orders, and so on.

Through the network, the practitioner can have "face-to-face" audio-visual contact with all functions of the health care community. Through whatever information appliance (e.g., videotex-augmented telephone, personal digital assistant, personal computer) available, the practitioner can tap into the hospital-stored data or expertise (communications hub) or into outside consulting services, databases, and decision assistance applications (via an information gateway). The data hub can provide unified communications for all patient care concerns; no matter where the service is rendered and no matter what health professional in the area renders it, multidirectional communication can take place. Some of the major locations from which access to the health care communication system will be available include

- hospital ward
- clinic
- doctor's office
- patient's home
- board-and-care home
- nursing home
- workplace
- school
- public access terminals (similar to public telephones with a video display)

The volume of transactions will allow the health care communications hub to provide innumerable auxiliary information services to practitioners and their clientele in a manner that is administratively automatic for the practitioner, as well as to operate at a fraction of the cost of the far more limited stand-alone practice-based systems. The hub will limit the amount of redundancy of specialized equipment and maintain the best quality telecommunication and peripheral technology. Expert staff members will set up, maintain, and teach practitioners how to use the system in a manner that is least time-consuming for the practitioners.

A complete digital record system will allow patient records to be electronically available at all times to the practitioner, whether he or she is calling in from the office, home, or someplace within the hospital facility. The digital record has a multiplicity of advantages over a paper chart; for example, Hypertext and Boolean database searches will allow access to significant positive and negative complaints over a lifetime or even cross-generationally. Trend analysis can be done quickly on virtually any numeric measure (e.g., changes in medication dosage or physiological measures such as blood pressure) over any specified amount of time.

Hospitals, durable medical equipment vendors, pharmaceutical companies, hospital supply companies, insurers, and home health care agencies are all beginning to develop their own information applications, many of which are linked to each other via telecommunication.[17] Several groups that have pioneered in using computers and telecommunication for improving the operations of their core businesses, such as American Hospital Supply, McKesson, and Blue Cross, are now beginning to facilitate new communications services with hospitals and practitioner groups; these new services represent new profit centers for these companies. Some of these services are transforming the delivery of health care and, in some cases, vastly improving the quality of care while substantially cutting the cost. For instance, pulmonary capacity measuring devices and similarly networked medical devices (e.g., fetal monitors) are making it possible to remove many of the traditional hospital functions out of the hospital to outpatient centers and the home.

Over the next decade and beyond, physician remote communication is likely to become far more common in cases that do not require the physician's physical presence. The equivalent of the hospital ward computer can be a totally separate repository for a patient's care outside the hospital's purview and will likely have some of its functionality within the public network. With the computerized community nursing concept, for example, the equivalent of a ward nurse functions apart from the hospital for patients who are being seen at home, in board-and-care homes, or in nursing homes. They monitor the patients through a network and feed data to central computers. Physicians can then review and respond to the patients' needs and care-giver actions from the site of their own choosing.

The health care industry as a whole must take the necessary actions soon to ensure the interconnectivity of all health sector data and communications for hospitals, medical centers, community clinics, and their "partners" in care. The use of an intelligent network allows these groups to provide better services for less than services cost each group individually. An interconnected, multifunction network that best addresses the needs of the health sector also mitigates the splintering of health services and associated information services. If the health care industry adopts a unified, proactive stance regarding telecommunication, transformative clinical and administrative advances (such as remote clinical viewing, automatic claims processing, the interactive lifetime health record, and advanced imaging) can be universally accessible within 15 years.

The United States now stands on the edge of major changes to the information infrastructure and national telecommunication policy. These changes will open up vast new opportunities for the health care industry to enter the Information Age economy and to improve patient care by applying the full power of computerization and telecommunication to clinical uses. As a result, the health care industry will evolve beyond the fragmentation of health information and communication that plagues the industry today.

Lifetime Health Record

The health record of the next decade will be very different from the health record of today. The chart is fast becoming a lifetime health record that includes multigenerational data. The chart of the near future is interactive and dynamic, with all the data linked through database management features.

As the 1990s proceed, the chart will become less and less a phenomenon of the physician, more and more a phenomenon of the well individual/patient. The chart will no longer reside in paper files in the physician's office and hospital, but in a computer that makes it accessible to authorized individuals throughout the health communication system. There will be no need for redundant data entry, as there is today when a single individual has multiple specialists or several different practitioners over time. Essentially all the functions that take place in all sites, even remote sites, can and should become entries into the chart, such as board and care, social services, self-care, tests, and monitoring. With access to health-oriented telecommunication applications in the home, workplace, school, etc., the individual will be the major user of the chart on a monthly, weekly, and, in some cases, daily basis.

One of the advantages of a more informed and involved public who have access to their own medical charts is a reduction in medical malpractice costs.[18,19] As patients become more involved in their care, fewer errors are made, communication increases, and the locus of responsibility shifts; all this reduces the liability burden of the physician and medical institution.[20,21] In the shift toward patient-accessible and patient-controlled health records, along with the movement from tort law toward contract law, the locus of responsibility finds a more productive balance between provider and patient.[22]

The lifetime health record will have segmented access. Normally, only the patient-authorized practitioner(s) or the patient personally will be able to gain entry to the main body of information in the chart. The physician or the patient is likely to give authorization for other health care workers to see portions of the chart for specific functions, however. Charts are also likely to have a pre-authorized emergency section for medical personnel who are properly credentialled. Identification numbers and activities, including person, date, and time, will be automatically recorded for every access and entry to the chart. There will be preconstructed nonsecure portions of the chart that allow only data entry or only entry and review as appropriate by attending health workers. Both the patient and the physician should be able to maintain sections of the record to which only they themselves have access.

When a patient is admitted to the hospital, data will be entered on the health record from all parts of the hospital:

- Admitting
- Radiology and imaging
- Pharmacy
- Records
- Wards and nursing
- Laboratory
- Pathology
- Billing
- Dietetics

Therefore, the physician has a complete medical record of the patient's hospital stay and the nonconfidential portions of the personal health record. The chart can be connected on-line to all functions in the hospital and its affiliated institutions. Many activities that are disjointed and time-consuming today can be automatically performed. For example, just by touching choices on the system's menu, the physician can automatically order a medication, check for possible side effects with other medications that the patient is taking, post the prescription on the chart, post the medication to the nurse's orders on the bedside terminal, activate the billing charge, and fill out the appropriate insurance claim. In turn, when the prescription is sent from the pharmacy, an inventory control system automatically notes the purchase, reviews the stock, and authorizes new orders if the stock is low.

Diagnoses will be automatically reported to the Centers for Disease Control (CDC). If the signs and symptoms or diagnosis are related to a current epidemic, the physician will be notified regarding the epidemic and given clinical briefings on how best to address the concerns of the patient. Names of individual patients will not be sent to the CDC—only locally encoded identification numbers.

In addition to internal hospital communication, the health care communications system can also play a role in organizing the entirety of services at all off campus sites such as the home, practitioners' offices, ambulatory care centers or other hospitals even in geographically distant areas.

Remote Monitoring

Some patients, such as women in early labor at home or patients recovering at home from myocardial infarction, may need remote monitoring. There are three modes in which remote monitoring can take place:

1. Live, real-time monitoring with the attending health care workers monitoring and interpreting the signals directly.
2. Monitoring in which data are stored for later review. Data may either be stored locally and periodically sent through the network for review or sent in real time and stored on the central computer.

3. Emergency-activated monitoring in which data are stored only on location, but, if a measurement goes outside of normal or specified limits, the on-location device automatically dials the emergency center connected to the system and notifies the attending physician.

In essence, this means that a patient at home or at some other remote site is observed and data are entered into the chart as if the patient were hospitalized. The attending physician simply enters the communication system at a local information appliance, examines the monitoring data, stores what is relevant, and orders treatment accordingly. Information and communications procedures are essentially the same from any location. They are simple enough to use so that allied health workers and lay care-givers do not make deadly mistakes. For example, a board-and-care nurse can study the insulin use of a diabetic patient over the past few years as administered and monitored by several practitioners.

Data review and decision making will be far more effective in emergency situations, such as on a road side, in an ambulance or plane, or at the scene of a crime, accident, or fire. Emergency room staff will be directly communicating with the on-site emergency personnel. Once fiber optic capability and digital radio transmission are available, remote evaluation and triage will greatly improve.

As the ISDN and fiber optics are installed into the public network, the health care communications hub will allow for face-to-face, on-line consultations for all local practitioners in real time. Thus, individuals in remote sites not only will be able to talk to each other as they do today over the telephone, but also will be able to see each other as they talk and, within their conversation, simultaneously review an X-ray, a laboratory result, or some other aspect of the patient's chart. Other practitioners, or even the patient, may be brought into their discussions at will by means of the ISDN's multichannel capabilities.

Reviewers from multiple locations will be able to study the results of electronic imaging, such as CT scans, positron emission tomography (PET) scans, and magnetic resonance imaging (MRI), at times and places convenient to the reviewers. If required, the radiologist will be able to explain and illustrate the pathological findings as though the two were in the same room. When it is necessary to involve specialty physicians from a geographically distant site in a procedure, they can provide a remote consultation through high-definition television. For example, a University of Texas specialist in cardiovascular surgery will be able to look in on a surgical procedure in a rural hospital in Northern Texas remotely, significantly cutting down on travel time and expense for consultation.[23] Similarly, the referring rural physician will be able to look through a laparoscope into the abdomen of a patient whom he has referred to Houston from the rural hospital.[24]

As the availability of high-definition television and its derivatives increases, the price:performance ratio will decrease. Physicians will use the same system to see laboratory specimens at a remote location or to look at a lesion on the leg of a patient in a board-and-care home, for example. In the next decade, a surgeon in the surgical suite may be able to look through a microscope, by means of high-definition television, at a specimen just sent to the pathology laboratory and discuss the specimen with the pathologist.[25] In some cases, the pathologist will be able to look back, via high-definition television, into the sterile field in the surgical suite and offer further advice about how to deal with any disease in the surrounding tissue.[26]

Impact of Emerging Technologies on the Practice of Medicine

Given the continuing growth of medical specialization and the increasing number of health-related professional categories, increased communication becomes critical. The fact that real-time "face-to-face" discussions over information appliances between two or more individuals will be able to occur much more readily than is possible today is likely to transform not only the operational aspects of patient care, but also its quality control and professional education. The ability to connect many medical experts, whether in the hospital or in remote locations, via both real-time and delayed (through databases, computer conferences, or electronic mail) communication will greatly enhance clinical outcomes by increasing the medical intelligence engaged to resolve difficult therapeutic problems.

Shortly after the turn of the twenty-first century, surgery will become quite different from surgery today. Most operations will be minimally invasive because of breakthroughs in telepresence, virtual reality, and microrobots. Instead of standing over the patient on the operating table, the surgeon will operate from what appears to be a black box away from the patient. This box, a virtual reality workstation, will allow the surgeon to look into the body and navigate through it visually. Once digitized, this telepresence/virtual reality surgical workstation will allow the surgeon to operate just as easily from across the state or nation as if he or she were in the same room.

In some cases, the surgeon will be able to see not only with stereoscopic vision at whatever magnification desired, but also will use artificially colored CT scans or MRI mathematically correlated with the real-time laparoscopic images in order to better observe and rectify the problem at hand. Using this composition of digital images (some in real time and some taken from previous imaging), the surgeon will manipulate workstation instruments connected digitally to microrobots within the patient's body. These instruments will allow the surgeon to feel the tissues cut and the tension on them, as well as to see the tissues in question.

Because the operation will be minimally invasive, involving a laparoscope and embedded robotic instruments introduced through four small ports (i.e., punctures in the skin and tissue), there will be less trauma and less chance of infection. In some cases, patients who undergo operations that now require 2 weeks for recovery will be up and walking around in 2 days. The operation will leave minimal or no scars. In addition, the use of stereoscopic microscopes, overlays of imaging data, and microrobotic equipment will increase the precision of the operation and substantially reduce the chances for error.

The communications network of the future will have significant advantages to the practitioner's office as well. The primary advantage for most practitioners will be that they can pay less attention to the tedious administrative functions of running an office and pay more attention to their patients. Through an information appliance in the office, they will be able to accomplish all of the following administrative functions through the health care network (many of them in a far more automated fashion than through distributed processing alone):

- Billing
- Patient records
- Reminders
- Appointment
- Drug prescription orders
- Supplies ordering
- Insurance claims
- Collections

Proper transaction structures will make it possible to manage the increasing burdens of utilization review and quality control much more effectively and, in most cases, proactively. Personnel training, including continuing medical education, and performance tracking will also take place through the system. Simulations that allow practitioners to perform procedures on simulated patients will allow them to sharpen their skills, to broaden their therapeutic experience far beyond what they can normally do in the usual practice environment, and to learn the limits and fine points of safe practice that they cannot explore with real patients where a mistake may cause unfortunate side effects or even death or disability.

The health care communication system must also act as a gateway to information from anywhere in the world. The system will keep abreast of and subscribe to all relevant network systems, either by being one of the National Library of Medicine's 5,000 affiliated hospitals or, if small, relating to one of them.[27] In turn, they will be tied to 120 research libraries or to a regional data center and the National Library of Medicine itself. As a result, any affiliate of the hospital-based information system can tap into any knowledge domain or expertise needed. Consequently, there will be a dramatic improvement in the quality of care.

Primary clinicians responsible for a nontypical case will be able to browse within the scientific and medical knowledge portions of the system and to locate national and international consulting experts who can help to resolve the problem at hand. Using the network for asynchronous work and communication may be the most efficient and productive. If unable to reach the consultant specialist directly on the first attempt, the primary clinician can post a detailed request, noting the level of urgency and providing the portions of the chart that the consultant practitioner will need. Then, the consultant can review the materials as soon as possible, post a reply, and arrange for a face-to-face communication, if necessary. In order to use their consulting time most efficiently, many specialists may refer the attending clinician to ongoing forums in the area of requested knowledge or to preconstructed materials, such as protocols, algorithms, simulations, or other knowledge sources (e.g., examining stills, videos of operations, graphic displays of specimens on line, exemplary laboratory results, statistics of similar cases) that the consulting specialists have compiled from their own research or clinical experience.

Who benefits from the health care communications hub? The health sector benefits through the resolution of some of its present problems with cost, quality of care, and distribution, as well as through the enhancement of its mandate for the 1990s and the twenty-first century. Hospitals and other health care institutions benefit through the generation of new profit centers and good will in the community. Physicians and other practitioners benefit through enhanced capability, reduced administration, and vastly improved communication and access to consulting expertise. Ultimately, however, the greatest beneficiaries will be the patients, especially those in the rural areas, who most lack access to state-of-the-art expertise and facilities.

Public Health

Traditionally, the term *public health* designates institutions that focus on

1. Measuring the health status of groups
2. Discovering patterns of illness in society
3. Determining the generative factors of disease
4. Intervening to alleviate the problem[28]

Traditional interventions include education, as well as biomedical and environmental measures, to improve the health of individuals, communities, and society in general.

Public health is beginning to take on a broader meaning because of shifts in culture, demographics, epidemiology, technology, and knowledge of health and human potential. This broader context encompasses action taken both by groups of individuals and by institutions directed at improving the public's health. These broader efforts can be considered a Public Health Movement.[29]

The Public Health Movement faces the challenges of many health-related problems, such as environmental degradation and substance abuse, that have been inadequately addressed to date. Many emerging health problems are too complex to be managed or prevented by health professionals and legislation alone. The actions of informed individuals, groups of concerned citizens, and communities play a critical role. Intrinsically democratizing electronic media are essential in unleashing the potentials of the Public Health Movement, because such media make it possible to build a system of participatory involvement in addressing public health problems during the decades ahead.

Some of the greatest emerging challenges to health are presently worsening conditions, and new methods will be required to manage them. In addition, it will be necessary to build the scientific, technological, and social framework to address the precursors to problems for which data are still scant. Many of these challenges to the public's health will necessitate on-line monitoring, multivariate analysis, and simulations that require better computer modeling, vastly faster transmission speeds, and interdisciplinary collaboration in the creation of broader knowledge bases than are available today. It is essential to plan ahead to improve communications during crises (e.g., earthquakes, hurricanes, toxic releases, the introduction of new street drugs) and epidemics (e.g., pediatric lead poisoning, AIDS, influenza), as well as to circumvent catastrophes, epidemics, or slowly deteriorating conditions.

For example, monitoring air and water quality provides important knowledge regarding the likelihood of outbreaks of lung and gastrointestinal diseases and conditions such as asthma, dysentery, and cancers.

Many existing monitoring systems (e.g., data collection on elevated levels of lead, mercury, formaldehyde, toluene, asbestos dust, and chemicals such as pesticides and herbicides) are too primitive to provide effective early warning, however. All too often, months, years, and, in some cases, decades go by before the rates of birth defects, advanced incurable disease, or deaths pinpoint the factors that underlie major health problems. Health-oriented telecommunication applications, whether for epidemiology, early warning, public education, or research, can lead to tremendous strides in protecting the public's health.

Epidemiological Studies and Early Warning

By observing the environmental conditions, life styles, and health status of large numbers of individuals and groups, it is possible to discover the relationships between health and combined factors of age, sex, race, access to care, use of transportation, habits, occupations, general environments, poverty, and education. The groups that are most susceptible to certain kinds of ill health often become obvious.[30] Genetic predisposition, environmental conditions, access to basic medical services, and life style are among the risk factors that indicate who is likely to fall victim to specific conditions.[31]

Today, physicians are required to report only specific contagious diseases and very few other conditions (e.g., child abuse, convulsions). Even with these few requirements, the reporting is so poor that decisions very often must be based primarily on intuition. Health-oriented telecommunications that allow cooperating clinicians to report certain conditions automatically as a part of the process of entering a diagnosis, sign, or symptom into a dynamic electronic medical record will greatly improve health policy and clinical decision making by uncovering patterns of health problems that today go unnoticed.

A system with automatic reporting features and improved routine multifactorial analysis can also reduce adverse outcomes. In a study of a system to monitor adverse drug effects in a Salt Lake City hospital,[32,33] for example, it was found that a specially programmed clinical system detected 60 times as many adverse drug effects as did the traditional methods. More than 95% of the adverse drug effects detected were moderate to severe and required a change in treatment regimen. This, of course, has major implications for efforts to reduce iatrogenic conditions, as well as to control costs and to maintain the quality of care. With integrated clinical and social service tracking systems, the synergistic effects of medical, genetic, life style, and environmental factors can be monitored, leading to earlier intervention on newly defined syndromes.

Because all health-oriented telecommunications encounters maintain confidentiality and privacy, data from the health risk assessment and health history sections of the personal health record, including a limited statement of known diseases and evidence of ill health and risks, can be automatically fed into local and regional data banks. The core data of these local and regional databases can be identically organized so that their data can be periodically uploaded for state-wide and national studies by the Public Health Service, CDC, and research centers of all kinds.

For purposes of surveillance, it may prove to be valuable to look for the human equivalent of *indicator species* (an environmental science term for a species of animal that is among the first to show the effect of an environmental degradation that has a broad impact on many species).[34] "Indicator populations" or "sentinel populations," such as crack babies, provide not only a sense of the frequency and spread of a given disease, but also insights into the health of the community within which indicator cases occur.

Multiple indicator conditions (e.g., prevalence of AIDS, teen-age homicide, and crack babies in the inner city populations) connote massive deterioration of the social environment. An imbalanced or rapidly changing social environment dramatically affects the quality of life of people in the surrounding areas as well, although their suffering may not be so apparent or sensational. Special attention can be paid to indicator cases, conditions, and populations in specific high-risk communities and geographical regions, for example, along the border with Mexico, to control for the transmission and migration of conditions such as yellow fever and cholera.[35] Indicator conditions, sentinel populations, and sentinel cases will be automatically recorded and analyzed at local or state health departments, as well as at the CDC, so that endemic conditions and disease invasion can be recognized.

Similarly, voluntary "sentinel networks" maintained on-line with people who are known to have a particular sensitivity to specific conditions may allow early identification and subsequent capture of etiologic agents, which, in the case of influenza, may call for the incorporation of new antigens into the annually antigenically reconfigured vaccine. One important sentinel network of growing importance is composed of people who suffer from environmental illness.[36,37] When exposed to small doses of toxic chemicals, these highly sensitive individuals develop symptoms such as severe headaches, nausea, reduced mentation, or diminished coordination. Their symptoms indicate a slow buildup of dangerous chemicals in the environment that does not yet affect the broader population, just as canaries stop singing and eventually lose consciousness before a decreased oxygen level in the coal mines affects miners.

It is very likely that analyzing large databases through the use of high-performance computers and new mathematical principles that can find nonlinear correlation and synergistic relationships among very complex datasets will yield many breakthroughs in understanding syndromes and diseases presently described as "of unknown etiology."[38] Diseases that are endemic, yet still undetected, may be identified and managed more effectively. Moreover, the kind of collateral information available may well point up origins or co-factors quite apart from the commonly postulated cause.

Environmental Monitoring

A health-oriented telecommunication system connected to optrodes (i.e., optical fiber with a biological or chemical sensor attached) can provide ongoing monitoring of environmental conditions that are difficult or expensive to measure by other data collection methods. Such monitoring has three purposes: (1) to measure specific environmental levels or changes for a specific locale involving a limited number of people, called a microapplication; (2) to measure these same levels in vast regions, even continents and the global environment, called a macroapplication; or (3) to identify breakdowns in traditional sanitation activities that lead to disease outbreaks.

Microapplications

Ongoing monitoring of a process or a facility that has a potential for dangerous materials leakage may identify potential Love Canals or Denora Valleys before they begin to affect the quality of human life or surpass other important environmental health thresholds. Any interested professional or layperson will be able to study the continuous data through environmental health databases accessed via the public network and common information appliances. If the level of any monitored substance exceeds an established threshold, an alarm will instantly notify the health or safety department to activate containment procedures.

In a current microapplication, the Contra Costa County Community Alert Network uses a combination of existing computer and telecommunication technologies to inform community members within specific ZIP code areas when they may be in danger because of emergencies such as chemical spills, earthquakes, fires, explosions, or prison escapes. Notification messages can be in different languages. They can carry standard messages to multiple households simultaneously or customized messages, as in an unanticipated event or in a rapidly changing situation.[39,40]

Macroapplications and Global Applications

As massive changes continue in population, pollution, and energy and other resource consumption, macroapplications of environmental monitoring have become infinitely important. These applications involve the on-line collection and analysis of data that relate to the precursors of apocalyptic change. Already there are indications of catastrophic damage to Earth's life support system, resulting in ozone layer depletion, acid rain, soil and water burdens, forest damage, and global climate changes. Because these types of problems may continue for decades even after interventions have begun to neutralize their adverse effects, early warning signs are essential.

Many types of measurements are being made to monitor the global environment, and many more are being planned for the coming decade within a national initiative called the Global Change Research Program. Just as physicians determine their patients' health by monitoring temperature, chemistry, circulation, and skin color, so do Earth scientists investigate the health of the planet by monitoring the global radiation budget, atmospheric and oceanic chemistry and circulation, and global greenness.

An improved telecommunication infrastructure that can provide scientists with a more straightforward access to present and future databases will greatly enhance human understanding of Earth's ecological system and its resiliency to stress. Poor access to existing data that are sitting in archives is already severly hampering environmental scientists in their modeling efforts. With telecommunication-aided monitoring, not only can data collected by scientists be more accessible to the public, the public can collect and add to databases. The National Aeronautics and Space Administration (NASA) recognizes this need as they plan for the implementation of their Earth Observing System.

Traditional Sanitation Breakdowns

Food sanitation breakdown, such as failure to maintain proper refrigerator temperatures for food and hot water temperatures for dishwashing lead to the transmission of food-borne illness. With an improved telecommunication system, these temperatures can be monitored, and an alarm can be set to go off should a temperature fall outside established limits. The health department can monitor these temperatures, either continuously or periodically, via the intelligent network.

Special Case Control

In several instances, special types of electronic surveillance may be useful for people who have certain types of health problems or whose actions may jeopardize the health or safety of others. For example, just as criminals who have committed violent crimes may be put on an electronic surveillance alarm during probation, people with records of driving under the influence of alcohol may have their vehicles fitted with a computerized sobriety test. They may have to pass a sobriety test before they can start the car. If the individual repeatedly fails the sobriety test, the system may send a message directly to the probation officer under special circumstances. Similarly, people with Alzheimer's disease or schizophrenia may be fitted with a bracelet monitor that notifies family members or health professionals when they stray beyond their designated safe zone. The same device may be used to find the individual who has gone beyond the safe zone.

As useful as these applications can be, public health professionals, concerned lay public, and scholars on civil liberties must be involved in discussing the ethics, broad implications, and proper restrictions of these types of applications. Although even limited electronic surveillance of those who drink and drive smacks of "Big Brother," this type of surveillance may be a desirable option for those individuals whose job and family's sustenance depend on their driving and whose only other option is the loss of their license and mobility.

Research Tool for Investigation of Disease Etiology

The personal health information system, as well as the dynamic lifetime medical record, provides unprecedented opportunities for gathering confidentiality-protected data on specific populations for research purposes. Because both the personal health information system and the public interest communication system and electronic library (PICSEL) can gather information as they deliver information, the collection of extensive data on the relationship between life style and environment, onset of illness, and progression of disease to resolution or death is feasible and cost-effective. Gathering such data from very large numbers of individuals in most subgroups in the United States will revolutionize health research and make it possible to do routine population studies and health analyses that cannot be done today because of the cost involved in traditional studies of this nature.

As the Public Health Movement shifts its focus toward community interventions, the number of variables and problem complexity make the task of properly evaluating outcomes and intervening scientifically nearly impossible through traditional methodologies. Trials like the multiple risk factor trial on heart disease have made it clear that, even after the expenditure of hundreds of millions of dollars, it is very difficult to understand or control all the variables involved in health status improvement. Data management, coupled with the sciences of complexity (e.g., use of the computer to accomplish complex multivariate analysis and simulations), will help to clarify the causes and cofactors of illness, health, and the healing process that are still hard to conceptualize in terms of mainstream public health. By using an interdisciplinary database and modeling and monitoring techniques, the contributions of multiple variables and their synergistic effects can be more easily followed, understood, and systematically addressed.

Public Education and Involvement

Low-cost, universally accessible, easy-to-use information appliances will make the health risk assessment and other health-oriented telecommunication applications available to everyone, whether children or seniors, whether rich or poor. Because health-oriented telecommunication tasks will be interactive, each person will receive information customized to meet his or her unique, immediate, and evolving health needs. Each time an inquirer interacts with the personal health information system, the data are stored in a lifetime health record. The result is an advancing awareness of susceptibilities and potentials.

PICSELs will change the nature of communications within communities, especially within communities that have traditionally been disenfranchised from the production of knowledge. PICSELs will spawn the development of community interdisciplinary knowledge bases. As a result, they will allow diverse groups to analyze the factors that affect the health and prosperity of their community and its subpopulations.

The computing capability of PICSELs provides hope for solving problems that have complex origins and have resisted centralized solutions (e.g., substance abuse, environmental degradation, teen-age pregnancy, and gang violence). Community health strategists will find powerful tools for data collection and analysis in the tracking and mapping systems within PICSELs. Understanding the underlying causes and cofactors of complex social problems leads to solutions.

PICSELs not only democratize the reception and production of knowledge, but also facilitate an upward vertical exchange of information between community members and decision makers. Over time, this exchange augments and improves the responsiveness of representative government. Interactive media such as SCARCnet (tobacco advocacy network) and ALCnet (alcohol advocacy network), for example, have helped citizens affect health-related policy. The broad participation of citizens in collectively influencing the destiny of their own community both increases self-esteem and improves the quality of life. This is one of the ultimate goals of health education and will be greatly enhanced by properly designed health communication systems.

APPENDIX NOTES

1. A. C. Hastings, J. Fadiman, and J. S. Gordon, *Health for the Whole Person* (Boulder, Colo.: Auburn House Publishing Co., 1978).
2. Ibid.
3. "To Your Health," *Wall Street Journal,* January 16, 1992, p. A1.
4. J. A. D. Anderson, C. Buck, K. Danaher, and J. Fry, "Users and Non-Users of Doctors—Implications for Self Care," *Journal of the Royal College of General Practitioners* 27, no. 176(1977):155–159.
5. Hastings, Fadiman, and Gordon, *Health for the Whole Person.*
6. M. D. McDonald, "A Videotex-Based Personal Health Information System," *MEDINFO 86 Proceeding,* October 1986.
7. M. D. McDonald, "The General Public/Health Information Interface and the Personal Health Information System," AAMSI *(American Association of Medical Systems and Informatics)* Proceedings, May 1986.
8. A. Gartner and F. Reissman, "Self-Help Models and Consumer Intensive Health Practice," *American Journal of Public Health.*
9. D. M. Vickery, H. Kalmer, et al., "Effect of a Self-Care Education Program on Medical Visits," *Journal of the American Medical Association* 150 921 (1983):2952–2956.
10. W. A. Myers, "Two Medical Worlds—Separate and Unequal," *Western Journal of Medicine* July 1991 p. 84.
11. J. A. D. Anderson, C. Buck, K. Danaher, and J. Fry, "Users and Non-Users of Doctors—Implications for Self Care," *Journal of the Royal College of General Practitioners* 27, no. 176(1977):155–159.
12. S. R. Garfield, "The Delivery of Medical Care," *Scientific American* 222, no. 4(1970):155–159.
13. *Worksite Health Promotion Information* (San Francisco: Bay Pacific Medical Center, 1985).
14. The Health Strategies Group, *Helping Ourselves to Health: The Self-Care Market in the United States* (Emmaus, PA: Rodale Press, 1983).
15. B. Tones, "Health Education and the Ideology of Health Promotion: A Review of Alternative Approaches," *Health Education Research* 1, no. 1(1986):3–12.
16. M. D. McDonald and S. A. Deane, "The Dimensions of Health Promotion Communications Technologies," AAMSI *(American Association of Medical Systems and Informatics) Proceedings,* May 1987.
17. J. Foley, "Blue Cross' Hybrid Remedy," *Communications Week* March 4, 1991.
18. President's Commission for the Study of Ethical Problems in Medicine and Biomedical Research, *Making Health Care Decisions: The Ethical and Legal Implications of Informed Consent in the Patient-Practitioner Relationship* (Washington, D.C.: U.S. Government Printing Office, 1982).
19. J. Green, "Minimizing Malpractice Risks by Role Clarification: The Confusing Transition from Tort to Contract," *Annuals of Internal Medicine* 109, no.3(1989):234–241.
20. "Hospital Ruled Liable for Boy's Affliction," *Pittsburgh Post-Gazzette,* November 17, 1987.
21. T. Bradley-Steck, "Local Physicians Held Responsible in Damage Claim," *Beaver County Times,* May 17, 1983, p. A1.

22. R. Epstein, "Medical Malpractice: The Case for Contract," *American Bar Foundation Research Journal* 1(1976):87–149.
23. W. R. Tirman, *The Elephant and the Blind Men: The Phenomenon of HDTA and Its Would-Be Stakeholders*, Program on Information Resources Policy, Harvard University, August 1990.
24. W. Eckerson, "Texas Hospital Tests HDTV Net for Remote Diagnosis," *Network World*, March 12, 1990, p. 4.
25. M. Gladwell, "HDTV Link to Let Pathologists Study Tissue from Miles Away," *The Washington Post*, July 3, 1989, Finance section, Final Edition.
26. R. J. Willcourt, "Medical Applications of HDTV" (Paper and comments presented at the 2nd Annual Conference and Exhibition on High Definition Television, Arlington, Virginia, February 1990), *HDTV Newsletter*, pp. 12–14.
27. U.S. Department of Health and Human Services, Public Health Service, National Institutes of Health, *National Library of Medicine Long Range Plan* (Bethesda, MD: 1986).
28. H. L. Blum, *Planning for Health*, 2nd Edition (New York: Behavioral Publications, 1981).
29. H. L. Blum, et al., *Improving the Public's Health: A Proposal for California* (California Public Health Association—North, 1990).
30. U.S. Public Health Service, *Healthy People: The Surgeon General's Report on Disease Prevention and Health Promotion* (Washington, D.C.: Department of Health and Human Services, 1990).
31. H. L. Blum, *Expanding Health Care Horizons*, 2nd Edition (Oakland, Cal.: Third Party Publishers, 1982), p. 37.
32. "Computer Detects Potential Drug Reactions in Hospital Patients," *Research Activities*, Agency for Health Care Policy and Research, N. 150, February 1992, p. 1.
33. D. C. Classen, S. L. Pestotnik, D. Evans, and J. P. Burker, "Computerized Surveillance of Adverse Drug Events in Hospital Patients," *Journal of the American Medical Association* 266, no. 20(1991):2847–2851.
34. "Shades of Green," *East Bay Express*, April 1991, p. 1.
35. D. Solis, "Spread of Cholera in Mexico Prompts Warning by U.S. to Areas along Border," *Wall Street Journal*, August 16, 1991, p. B3D.
36. S. Coffel and K. Feiden, Eds., *Indoor Pollution* (New York: Fawcett Columbine, 1990).
37. G. Cohen and J. O'Connor, *Fighting Toxics* (Washington, D.C.: Island Press, 1990).
38. H. R. Pagels, *The Dreams of Reason: The Computer and the Rise of the Sciences of Complexity* (New York: Bantam Books, 1988).
39. T. McGlone, "Train Derailment, Spill of Chemical Sparks Evacuation," *Schenectady Gazette*, October 13, 1989.
40. T. L. Hein, "Community Notification Systems: No One Can Use Just One," EMEX 92 (*International Emergency Management Exposition and Conference*), San Francisco, March 17–19, 1992.

Discussion Summary

Michael McDonald (President, Windom Health Enterprises) noted that although television will be the dominant medium in the future, it will be very different from what it is today. He also said that he believes the future in terms of health information systems is likely to emerge in fits and starts with communications and computer applications as the major catalysts.

The "Age of Telecognition" will mean an increase in computing and information access and processing leading to a "dynamic" medical record.

According to David Feffer (Chairman, Employee Managed Care Corporation), the physician-based biomedical context traditionally used to treat disease is changing to one of patient-centered medicine. This new approach will contain four new components: (1) prevention, (2) self-care, (3) the patient–medical team partnership, and (4) the individual as case manager. The demand and capacity for this approach is growing daily; the only reason that it is not yet universally applied is that the knowledge skills required have not been universally available. Several medical practitioner organizations have already begun to support their members in acquiring such skills, however. Virtually all individuals have the capacity to manage their own health care if they are given the necessary tools and information, and are empowered to use them. Because motivation is so high, all that is now required are consumer-friendly systems. It is important not to relinquish individual responsibility to technology.

Michael Kahn (Assistant Professor of Medicine, Washington University) commented that there are no barriers to the ubiquitous computing and communications described by McDonald. All the pieces are already in place; what is missing is a national will to apply them.

Because the gestational period for new microprocessors is approximately 18 months, there will be some 19 generations over the next 30 years. Since these processors will produce billions and billions of bytes, the age of telecognition will present several challenges. Kahn noted first the need to identify, abstract, and save only the significant data. This is an important decision, because it limits the data that will be continuously available and, thus, the questions that can be asked. Second, data quality and integrity must be considered. Data that are gathered, but not used, are useless; similarly, data that are not used quickly become useless. Third, if computers are to work together, they must be able to exchange concepts among themselves. This raises the question of the language that is to be used between computers. Finally, with billions and billions of bytes, it is necessary to determine where precisely to look for knowledge. The proximity of data must not be confused with its productivity (i.e., its usefulness). The National Library of Medicine has a project in which it is attempting to codify the location of knowledge. Similarly, such systems as the "Knowbots" of Robert Kahn and Passive Information Grazers (PIGs) are agents that look for information. These will become common and widely used.

With 'billions and billions' of bytes, it is necessary to determine where precisely to look for knowledge.

One participant disputed the assumption that all the necessary technology for McDonald's scenario is currently available. Implantable sensors, for example, are available though they have not yet been successful in the long term. The basic problem (beyond the fact that his paper forecasts technology over the next 30 years), McDonald suggested, may be that science develops these technologies and then goes on to another technology before the next logical, post-development step in the manufacture of such devices is carried out thereby assuring a durable effect. Basic research is still required. The question of who is going to pay for development remains unanswered, however. If insurance companies, for example, do not cover new technological products, small companies cannot afford development investment.

The emphasis on personally-managed health care may cause problems for individuals who are incapable of self-care. Drug addicts may rationally know what is in their own interests, but might still make self-destructive decisions. As Feffer said, some highly motivated people do not need and do not want assistance in making their own decisions, while others are incapable of making well thought out decisions or prefer to rely on experts to tell them what to do. Most people, however, want at least some degree of control over their own lives. Motivation for self-care may depend in part on having some degree of control over outcomes.

In discussing the question of whether new drugs will become available much more rapidly in the future, Clement Bezold made the following observations. The medical environment will be radically different. The personal biochemical databases that result from noninvasive body function monitoring will become part of individual health records and will provide a broad database far superior to the one that is now garnered through clinical trials. The FDA is likely to seek information from drug companies, as well as large health care providers such as Kaiser Permanente. The greatly increased ability to model and simulate the actions of new drugs within the body will speed up Phases 1 and 2 of the FDA's testing process for new drugs. It also will be easier to track drugs *after* approval, something that is not being done well now. Again, this is a question of political will rather than a question of technology. There will continue to be some Phase 3 testing, although less than takes place now; many more data will be captured and quickly used in Phase 4. Many of these developments will be consumer-driven.

Dick Gourley (Professor and Dean, College of Pharmacy, University of Tennessee) raised the issue of the effect of ethics and litigation on these developments. The thalidomide disaster makes it clear that caution and safeguards for the public are essential. The public does not see any urgency in the approval of new drugs, with the possible exception of drugs that may be useful in the treatment of patients with terminal disease, such as AIDS, and is unlikely to accept any relaxation in safety standards. Moreover, in the area of pediatrics, there is little information available on the correct medications and correct dosages for some diseases. Gordon Klein (Associate Professor of Pediatrics, University of Texas) expressed a concern that speeding up the approval of drugs will leave the health care of children even further behind.

McDonald pointed out in response to these concerns that safety standards need not be relaxed if scientists take advantage of the powerful computer simulations that will be available to determine drug effects. In addition, education of health care practitioners must help them remain current with technological developments.

The real benefit of future technology in regard to the approval of drugs may be not in shortening the length of time required for the approval process, according to Schondelmayer, but in salvaging drugs that have been discarded because they have had one adverse effect or because their appropriate use is not clear. Instead of making decisions about drugs in the early stages, when the least information about the drug is available, the FDA is likely to have an ongoing approval process in which new indications and adverse consequences can be added much more efficiently.

This discussion led to a poll of the participants on the plausibility of changes in the drug approval process by 2020. A large majority believed that approval based primarily on post-marketing data will occur only in the case of drugs needed for life-threatening diseases for which there is no other treatment. Most believed that microchips and computer technology will be used to speed up the current process, though some believed that the drug approval process is likely to remain the same.

A change that is likely to shift the nature of the debate may come from biochemically unique, endogenous drugs. If these chemicals, similar to those developed in some current experimental therapies in which cancer patients are treated with vaccines genetically engineered from their own cancer cells, become the basis of medical treatment in the future, Jerome Halperin (Executive Director, United States Pharmacopeial Convention, Inc.) suggested that the drug approval process as we know it today may be moot. Sharon Northup (Director of Toxicology, Baxter Healthcare) pointed out that the FDA may have no authority to regulate such chemicals. It may be necessary to have a variety of types of regulation, one that fits "personally grown" individual treatments and another more conventional one that applies to drugs used for large populations. Some participants felt that the FDA's future role may have to be in regulating the safety, rather than the efficacy, of drugs.

According to another participant, most people assume that government drug regulation is going to remain very important. It is possible, however, that managed care plans will become more important than the FDA. Government regulation will be irrelevant if the medical system does not adopt the drug; thus, decisions about the inclusion of a drug in formularies will be much more significant than government regulatory decisions.

A set of perhaps 200 private formularies is emerging; Coile postulated that this number will probably become only two or three dozen. These formularies may contribute to the conduct of "Phase 5" clinical trials on the actual use of pharmaceuticals, including the off-label uses.

On the issue of cost and resource use for a health-oriented telecommunication system such as that described by McDonald, Feffer noted that there are reliable data indicating that the cost of care decreases and the quality and appropriateness of care increase with additional consumer-driven information. Health care providers are likely to find that investment in their information infrastructure is essential if they are to be competitive. Diagnosis-related groups, for example, changed the strategic role of many hospital information systems. Some participants felt that the marketplace for information serviceware will increase dramatically, providing an additional source of funds as consumers purchase fewer traditional pharmaceuticals and begin to buy new information devices.

Some participants doubted the ability of the public to determine risks, claiming that publishing the track record of a drug would lead to its removal from the market. Others noted that patients are remarkably adept at making decisions when they are given the appropriate information in the appropriate manner. Questions also remain about the potential provider-bias.

ADDITIONAL COMMENTS

Comment on "Health in the Age of Telecognition" By Michael D. McDonald

By Donald R. Bennett, M.D., Ph.D.
American Medical Association
Chicago, Illinois

I would like to present some of my own assumptions and futuristic views and then contrast them with those proposed in Michael McDonald's discussion paper, "Health in the Age of Telecognition."

1. The remarkable health-oriented tools needed to predict, prevent, diagnose, and treat disease at the molecular level described by Stuart Davidson in "Medicines and Health Technology Through 2020" will indeed become available.

As a young biologist and then as a physician, one of my favorite stories revolved around the concept that the preface for all emergency manuals should contain a section entitled "What To Do until the Molecular Biologist Arrives." Well, like McDonald, I believe that the molecular biologist has arrived; after reading his paper, however, I would now add the words *and computer scientist* after molecular biologist.

2. The highest quality care for any individual is the most cost-effective care.

A theme of this discussion paper is that a health information system will maximize the individualization of health care management; therefore, the corollary of cost-effective care should be achieved. The proposed advances listed in the paper, such as self-care, computerized patient records, and the personal health information system, are essential elements of individualized care. By 2020, individual metabolic profiles for exogenous chemicals should be available so that many serious predictable adverse drug reactions will be preventable.

> **"By 2020, individual metabolic profiles for exogenous chemicals should be available so that many serious predictable adverse drug reactions will be preventable."**

3. We value human life more than anything else.

Because of this belief, society demands a higher level of competence from physicians than from those in most other occupations. Thus, it is understandable that society, professional associations, or government agencies have initiated a whole series of audit procedures (e.g., recertification processes, utilization reviews). McDonald proposes that even more credentialling and simulation training will become the norm in continuing medical education.

McDonald also has forecast that machines will dramatically enhance human intelligence and even that machines will be trusted much more than human "jellyware" to provide the right diagnosis and management. It may be expected that I, as a physician, could never support the futuristic vision of a "Robodoc" that replaces the judgment of a physician. Probably to the dismay of some of my colleagues, I support that concept, however. Only the computer will be capable of correlating and comparing the massive amounts of data that will be available, especially in the time frame required to individualize diagnosis and management.

Obviously, the judgment of a physician will still be necessary, but that judgment will likely be used much more in the deliberative model than in the paternalistic model of the physician-patient relationship. In other words, the physician will probably serve as a friend and teacher rather than as a guardian. The physician's judgment will be especially important when the physician must explain the reason for a medical decision to a patient or family, particularly when societal needs outweigh individual needs.

4. The ready availability of an effective tool may bear little relation to its use or usefulness.

In the late 1960s, there were five to ten classes of antihypertensives available, but they were not being utilized to their fullest extent. It required an educational program of national proportions, the stepped-care program, to capture the attention of both physicians and patients, and to promote their appropriate use of readily available agents. Similarly, oral contraceptives have been with us for a quarter of a century, but a desirable rate of growth of the world population has not been achieved. Thus, I am concerned about the timely realization of the benefits of health information systems that McDonald describes in his paper. Physicians have been slow, if not reluctant, to utilize the computer for professional reasons.

5. Major goals of a health information system are to educate and to persuade appropriately.

I strongly agree that the Public Interest Communications System and Electronic Library (PICSEL) is an appropriate system to achieve the goals of a health information system, particularly in the area of self-care. In my opinion, if the PICSEL is to be of optimum benefit, a stricter code of advertising practices must mute or revise the counterforce of even subtle promotion from commercial health care advertising. If we are to shift, as McDonald suggests, from a physician-patient to a patient–drug information system, I, for one, would like to be assured that the patient is using the PICSEL system rather than relying solely on a commercial system for the information.

6. The standards for drug information must have a greater margin of acceptable error than do the standards for drugs, devices, procedures, and techniques.

Standards in biology and medicine have always required a greater margin of acceptable error than do standards in the chemical and physical sciences. Factors such as emotional response, attitude toward behavioral change, and level of educational competence vary considerably among individuals; therefore, our colleagues in the more mathematically precise disciplines will have to remain patient with us even in the year 2020.

I compliment Mr. McDonald on providing us with an excellent paper to stimulate discussion.

Comment on "Health in the Age of Telecognition" By Michael D. McDonald

By Gregory M. Fahy, Ph.D.
American Red Cross
Rockville, MD

Michael McDonald's vision of the future is a decentralized system of medical care in which every patient will be not only a recipient, but also a *provider* of information. The exchange of information will be interactive, comprehensive, and fast. It will allow optimized attention to the needs of each individual patient and will greatly streamline decision making by regulatory and standards-setting bodies. Indeed, decision making itself may be automated to a considerable extent, in part because humans will be too slow in the face of an accelerating avalanche of information, in part because of public demand, and in part because the huge information input to the network will make trends discernible much sooner via automatic data-tracking mechanisms.

I essentially agree with McDonald's general vision. Computer networks exist already. Hypertext companies such as Xanadu in Silicon Valley are creating interactive media today. The magazine *Longevity* is already setting up a system of patient data pooling to accelerate the development of interventive gerontology. Because, in my opinion, most human problems result from inadequate information, the power of McDonald's virtually inevitable net can hardly be overstated. As he implies, the question of who will write the software for the net is directly relevant to this audience. I cannot speak to the mind-machine link-ups that McDonald has proposed, except to say that what seemed implausible to me at first seemed less implausible when I reflected on systems that already have been shown capable of representing letters of the alphabet in the visual fields of blind people via link-ups between electrodes, computers, and television cameras.

As important as McDonald's information network is, its effectiveness will ultimately be limited by the therapeutic agents available. Some of the most powerful of these may very well be products of nanotechnology. McDonald refers variously to "nanodevices," "biochips," and even to "nanocomputers" and "implantable surgical robots." Let me clarify what nanotechnologists mean by such ideas.

Today's manufacturing technologies are essentially bulk technologies: vast assemblages of molecules are manipulated in statistical herds rather than individually. Long before the end of the next century, this situation will be reversed. Through nanotechnology, it will be possible to control the structure of matter atom by atom or molecule by molecule and, thus, to make essentially anything that is not forbidden by physical law. This will be done by means of artificial molecular machines.

Presently, molecular machines known as ribosomes are used to make all the proteins in the biosphere. Ribosomes are essentially programmable, all-purpose protein assemblers. By supplying them with new mRNA "tapes" and artificial transfer RNAs, molecular engineers will be able to co-opt ribosomes to allow the synthesis of complex manipulative tools for constructing still more versatile and convenient molecular machines. The use of transfer RNAs outfitted with molecule-sized machine parts (e.g., bearings or structural support struts) in place of amino acids could allow self-assembly of almost any device desired.

What are possible examples of products that could be made by advanced, programmable molecular machines? Nanocomputers that store information in the positions of sliding rods could store 1,000 megabytes per cubic micron and operate at 10^{10} operations per second. A sugar cube–sized computer based on these components would possess 200 billion times the storage ability of today's high-end personal computer and would operate more than 100 million times faster than today's fastest supercomputers. Other molecular machines could identify human immunodeficiency virus (HIV) components and disassemble them into nucleic or amino acids. These possibilities could transform drugs into programmable devices with sensory, decision-making, and effector capabilities that might overcome the so-far unavoidable problems of existing drugs, such as side effects and allergic reactions. Designed "smart pharmaceuticals" might activate themselves only when, where, and if needed. When combined with the therapeutic agents derived from conventional biotechnology, they could eradicate virtually any disease and might also make serious inroads into aging. Meanwhile, some nanomachines will be cleaning up the environment, while others replace conventional dirty technologies with manufacturing methods that are as clean and quiet as those used by trees and cats.

Viewed from the perspective of today's technology, nanotechnology may appear to be a sophomoric fantasy. It is not. Nanotechnology is virtually inevitable, and it will ultimately constitute perhaps the greatest technological revolution in history. Already, the Japanese Ministry of International Trade and Industry (MITI) is building the world's first Nanotechnology Center in Tokyo; MITI and Stanford University have sponsored meetings devoted to nanotechnology; and Xerox has begun its own nanotechnology research program. Admiral David Jeremiah, Vice Chairman of the Joint Chiefs of Staff, has also stressed the importance of nanotechnology for the defense of the United States.

> **"Nanotechnology is virtually inevitable, and it will ultimately constitute perhaps the greatest technological revolution in history."**

However, the biggest unknown is timing. The year 2020 is only 28 years away. Scientists are already designing artificial enzymes and are manipulating individual atoms with scanning tunneling microscopes. Global competition for the creation of smart pharmaceuticals could become intense, particularly given the reality of much of McDonald's molecular modeling software now and the facilitating effects of enthusiastic traffic on his health-oriented telecommunication nets in the future. It is, therefore, likely that at least some of the health information that McDonald has described will indeed be about injectable robots and biochips before the year 2020.

4

Medicines and Health Technology Through 2020

by Stuart N. Davidson
Director, Center for Technology Assessment
St. Joseph Health System
Orange, California

Through fresh intellectual constructs and an international and interacting system of scientific research, today's new sciences are rapidly developing the tools needed to predict, prevent, diagnose, and treat disease at the molecular level with degrees of certainty heretofore deemed impossible. These accomplishments, by forcing us to make choices from a veritable cornucopia of new approaches to disease, will engender continuing dramatic changes in the practice of medicine, the sites of medical care delivery, and the personnel needed at those sites. The task of clinically applying the wondrous results of non-Cartesian sciences to the chaotic cardiovascular, cognitive, pulmonary, nervous, digestive, and immunological systems of humans will be daunting—but doable.

By the year 2020, the routine clinical use of new generations of ultrasensitive imagers; biosensors, including DNA chips; monoclonal antibodies of ever-increasing sensitivity and specificity; the chain reaction analyzers; and highly technical, but simplified, test kits of all descriptions will bring an era of unprecedented diagnostic certainty (although never 100% certainty). In therapeutics, the clinical use of colony-stimulating factors, interleukins, interferons, a wide variety of human growth factors, and monoclonal antibody–based diagnostics will usher in an era of therapeutic certainty to match the newly blossoming diagnostic certainty—both by 2005. New additions to the medical armamentarium will include adoptive or individualized cancer chemotherapies; genetic vaccines; monoclonal antibody–based therapeutics; antisense drugs; transcription factors; taxol and other nature-made, but human-modified or human-synthesized, drugs; and other drugs from among the limitless possibilities that arise from the application of molecular dynamics. Most of these are already at least in early research stages.

The disease-free planet will be a technological possibility. The evolution of that possibility into a probability, or even a reality, is a question for sociologists, philosophers, and others rather than a science generalist.

THE SCIENCES

During the first half of the seventeenth century, Rene Descartes developed a philosophy that is now known as the Cartesian view. He held that the universe is composed of microscopic corpuscles (called atoms today) and that all natural phenomena can be explained in terms of their shape, size, and motion. Together with the work of Sir Isaac Newton, which was published later in the seventeenth century, and others, the work of Descartes formulated the scientifically accepted views of matter, energy, time, and light until well into the twentieth century. This view of the universe has proved totally inadequate, by itself, to deal with the miracles of nature as they are now understood, however. Since the 1930s, entirely new scientific constructs (e.g., information theory, fractal geometry, chaos theory, molecular dynamics, molecular biology, and nonlinear dynamics) have been developed to explain the miracles that are unexplainable from the Cartesian view.

Newton, when praised for his great scientific achievements, demurred by saying that he stood upon the shoulders of the giants who came before him (e.g., Galileo Galilei). In the time of Descartes and Newton, however, it often took years for a new piece of original scientific thought or experiment to reach other scientists. The "giants" moved slowly. In today's world of science, through the use of newsletters, technical journals, air travel, computer networks, electronic mail, and the now ubiquitous fax machine, widely scattered research teams stand on each others' shoulders in real time.

THE MOLECULAR NATURE OF DISEASE†

Some researchers have described the genetic mechanisms underlying myotonic dystrophy, a common form of adult muscular dystrophy.[1–5] Other researchers have found commonalities in the molecular genesis of two different diseases, Fragile X syndrome[6–7] and spinal bulbar muscular atrophy.[8] As it turns out, their molecular genesis is also similar to that of myotonic dystrophy. In lay terms, all three are caused by "stuttering genes" that repeat themselves unnecessarily.

These research efforts (and hundreds of others) make it reasonable to intuit that genetic diseases may have similar molecular pathways. But can this also be possible for the hosts of infectious diseases? According to an editorial in *Science*,

> All the bacterial toxins act in the same way; one component of the toxin is an enzyme that does the dirty work inside the cell, while the other components work to get the toxic component inside.[9]

> **"These research efforts (and hundreds of others) make it reasonable to intuit that genetic diseases may have similar molecular pathways."**

Like genetic, bacterial, and viral diseases, autoimmune disorders have common molecular pathways. In mid-1990, researchers developed a hydroxy urea compound called 64077 that binds selectively to 5-lipoxygenase. The drug was designed to inhibit this enzyme's ability to break down arachidonic acid into leukotrienes. The presence of leukotrienes in excessive amounts is a proximal cause of ulcerative colitis. An unrelated study showed that leukotrienes, also produced in the breakdown of arachidonic acid by 5-lipoxygenase, contribute to the molecular mechanism of asthma. Thus, two diseases previously considered totally different have a similar molecular genesis.[10]

Two enzymes, creatine phosphatase and lipoxygenase, have been found to play a role in the development of post-trauma brain swelling

---

† *Sections marked with † are derived substantially from S.N. Davidson, "System 2020 AD," St. Joseph Health System, Orange, California (publication pending). Used with permission.*

(cerebral edema). Because the concentration of creatine phosphatase correlates with the degree of brain damage in a trauma victim, measurements of creatine phosphatase levels are helpful in diagnosis. Lipoxygenase causes an overproduction of leukotrienes, producing the inflammation that leads to high intracranial pressure, loss of oxygen, and death or severe impairment as a result of brain trauma. This work was, incidentally, the first indication that the brain can produce its own inflammatory mediators.[11]

The recognition that disease is a molecular process accelerates science's ability to develop diagnostic technologies that may lead to both early and even predictive diagnoses. There will still be imperfections in the diagnostic processes, however, because each human has a unique biology and each human body, except on the autopsy table, is chaotic.

The Diagnostic Technologies

The Imagers

Medicine's most remarkable visualizing technology, the magnetic resonance imager (MRI), involves the manipulation of magnetic field gradients to reconstruct a two-dimensional image of soft tissues and malignant growth in vivo. Other imaging modalities, such as computerized tomography (CT), ultrasound, positron emission tomography (PET), and single photon emission computed tomography (SPECT), have become well established within their own niches. The diagnostic uses of MRI are still expanding into new areas, however. For example, recent advances in scanning speed, along with improved contrast agents for human use, have resulted in high-resolution in vivo brain studies that were previously impossible with MRI.[12] In addition, it has been found that magnetic resonance angiography accurately depicts flow phenomena in blood and cerebrospinal fluid,[13] and this technique is likely to replace conventional angiography.

Just as MRI provides anatomic information, magnetic resonance spectroscopy (MRS) provides a complete biochemical analysis. A prototype dual MRI/MRS device is now being developed for breast imaging.

This device will furnish not only anatomic images, but also spectrographic analysis of the breast tissue so that the biochemical composition of suspected tumors, and thus, the probability of their malignancy, can be determined. Such combined imager/spectrographic chemical analyzers will become centerpieces of the diagnostic centers of the future. When applied to biochemical samples, they can provide vital data about the structure of complex biological components such as enzymes, growth factors, and the 75,000 different protein molecules in the body, along with anatomic images of tissues and organs.

By the next decade, a new variation in MRI, echoplanar imaging, will provide high-resolution images at speeds of 30 frames per second, or at least 1,000 times faster than presently available MRI devices.[14] This technique has no motion artifacts, is free of ionizing radiation, and gives the operator free choice of image-plane orientation. The freezing of all anatomic motion permits clear images of areas that are often blurred by fluid flow and involuntary movements in images taken with slower methods.

Chain Reactions†

Essentially an amplifier of DNA, "the polymerase chain reaction (PCR) has dramatically altered how molecular studies are conducted as well as what questions can be asked."[15] A fragment of DNA is placed in a reaction bottle with a special enzyme called DNA polymerase. If put through a series of temperature cycles, the DNA polymerase causes the sample DNA to reproduce itself. A very few molecules of the DNA under investigation can become trillions in a short time. Thus, the PCR provides the laboratory technician with a large enough sample to perform many chemical analyses that were not possible in the past because the samples then available were too small for existing measurement technologies.

In conjunction with new generations of imagers and biodevices, the PCR's clinical use will make widespread certainty of diagnosis a possibility for the first time in the history of medicine. New diagnostic applications of the PCR are appearing almost daily. For example, the

† *Sections marked with † are derived substantially from S.N. Davidson, "System 2020 AD," St. Joseph Health System, Orange, California (publication pending). Used with permission.*

PCR's sample amplification capabilities make it possible to identify bacterial, fungal, and viral pathogens far earlier and more accurately than do presently used methods. In addition, the procedure permits a rapid genetic analysis of the unborn through an examination of a drop of the mother's blood rather than through an invasive and sometimes dangerous technique such as amniocentesis. According to a Johns Hopkins estimate, by 1995 the PCR will account for 90% of the DNA diagnostic methods for diseases caused by a single gene.

> Cystic fibrosis, a relatively common recessive genetic disease, was the first newly discovered gene to have its disease-causing mutation confirmed by PCR.[16]

Researchers on the project declared that, without the PCR, they would still have decades of work ahead. Like a previous amplification technology, the microscope, the PCR will significantly alter the course of science and medicine. "The raw power of PCR is awesome."[17]

Although the PCR amplifies a DNA sample that is cycled through it, the actual analysis takes place through a conventional laboratory instrument (e.g., a gas chromatograph), and determining the exact sequence of the amplified segment requires subsequent restriction enzyme analysis or DNA sequencing. A complementary technique, called the ligase chain reaction (LCR), permits the simultaneous detection and amplification of the sought after substance. In the long term, the LCR may replace the PCR, but is unlikely to do so for another 10 years (i.e., 2005, more or less).

Biosensors†

The clinical laboratories of the future will inevitably include in their inventories revolutionary biosensor devices developed from biochemistry, electronics, and the computer sciences.[18] Because biosensors are actually "chips," electronics firms or consortia of bioscience and electronic organizations may become the chief suppliers of these devices.

Biosensors, which have great potential as highly reliable money and time savers, will be available to duplicate many of the body fluid and

---

† *Sections marked with † are derived substantially from S.N. Davidson, "System 2020 AD," St. Joseph Health System, Orange, California (publication pending). Used with permission.*

tissue analyses presently done by other methods in today's clinical laboratory. The basic elements of such devices are generally biosubstances from a wide variety of sources, both natural and synthetic. For example, sugar beet cells may be used to detect tyrosine; cucumber leaf, to detect cysteine; rabbit liver, to detect guanine; and powdered rabbit muscle, to detect and measure adenosine monophosphate. A pH meter uses two metal electrodes to measure the acidity of a solution (e.g., blood pH, a standard clinical test). The sensors themselves are, of course, very small, often molecular in dimension.

"Biosensors, which have great potential as highly reliable money and time savers, will be available to duplicate many of the body fluid and tissue analyses recently done by other methods in today's clinical laboratory."

These sensors are electrically connected to transducers that convert physiochemical or electrochemical inputs from the sensor into electrical signals for transmission to a readout device or computer for handling and translation into information. The tests can be done in real time in the surgical suite, in the emergency room, at the bedside, and later at home. They will probably first be sited in clinical laboratories for in vitro tests,[19] but one hand-held analyzer is already under test at the University of Pennsylvania as a bedside monitor. The accuracy of measurements is already nearly as good as that of test results from the hospital's clinical laboratory,[20] and these biosensors will eventually allow inexpensive monitoring for any disease.

A laboratory biosensor developed for the human genome mapping project will probably evolve between 2010 and 2020 into the ultimate biosensor. Called a "DNA chip," this biosensor is an array of short pieces of DNA of known structure arranged on a substrate, or sensing surface. When a solution that contains the segment of DNA under study is splashed onto the chip, the pattern of the solution's DNA segment in relation to the known pattern of the immobilized DNA segments on the chip is revealed. By means of sophisticated mathematics and a very high speed computer, it is possible to determine the previously unknown structure of the DNA segment in the solution at a speed more than 100 times faster than that of existing technologies.[21–23]

Because such devices may be a quantum leap forward in clinical analyses, research grants are being awarded for the further development of these tiny devices. The project is likely to lead to the production of commercial applications for what will be called the "genosensor." Companies outside the project are already working on advanced versions of these devices. The ultimate result, perhaps by 2010, may be a complete clinical laboratory on a chip.

Chromosome Painting†

In a new laboratory technique, called chromosome painting, specific chromosomes are marked with molecules bearing unique and distinctive fluorescent characteristics. Long cultures are not needed, because the distinct colors appear in less than 24 hours. Furthermore, the process can probably be automated by the use of high-resolution microscopes, ultrasensitive detection cameras, and image analysis software.

Chromosome painting has been tested as a method of detecting birth defects through genetic analysis of a pregnant mother's blood sample and has been shown to be effective. With DNA probe technology, it is possible to complete the tests in 2 days as opposed to 1 to 3 weeks by cytogenetic analysis. In addition, because of the risks of miscarriages and other problems associated with amniocentesis and chorionic villus sampling, chromosome painting is likely to make these currently used procedures obsolete.[24]

In the area of cancer therapy, the technique of chromosome painting facilitates accurate diagnosis in the early stages of the disease so that the course of treatment can be initiated at a time when the chance of recovery is greatest. Joe Grey stated that "the era of individualizing

---

† *Sections marked with † are derived substantially from S.N. Davidson, "System 2020 AD," St. Joseph Health System, Orange, California (publication pending). Used with permission.*

cancer treatment is just beginning. Our research is going in the direction of understanding the evolutionary progression of tumors and hopefully identifying features that will permit therapy to be individualized."[25]

TODAY'S BIOTHERAPEUTIC TECHNOLOGIES†

Research scientists using such new tools as molecular genetics, computational chemistry, molecular dynamics, modern mathematics, and high-speed computer modeling of molecules are ushering in a new age in the design of biotherapies undreamed of only a few years ago. During the last decade of this century, the clinical use of these tools will make it possible to undertake the cure of disease rather than the treatment of its symptoms.

> **"The clinical use of these tools will make it possible to undertake the cure of disease rather than the treatment of its symptoms."**

Colony-Stimulating Factors (CSFs)

A wide variety of cytokines, called colony-stimulating factors (CSFs), boost production of white blood cells and are coming into clinical use for cancer treatment. For example, it appears that granulocyte macrophage–colony-stimulating factor (GM–CSF), which is being used to improve the immune systems of patients who are undergoing bone marrow transplantation, "may allow intensification of chemotherapy either by increasing the dose or decreasing the interval between courses of therapy."[26] As a result, patients will need less medication and will be able to go home sooner. Clearly, the use of CSFs is a cost-effective approach to cancer therapy.

Granulocyte–colony-stimulating factor (G–CSF), another genetically engineered immune system booster, sharply increases the number of granulocytes available to fight the infections to which chemotherapy patients are susceptible. Like other CSFs, however, it is an adjunct to cancer therapy—not a treatment for the cancer itself.[27]

Human Growth Factors

As this century's chronic diseases come under control and this society becomes increasingly mechanized and violent, the treatment of wounds may be a major concern of health care providers (along with stress-induced diseases). Until recently, modern medicine had not yet begun to devise treatments that actively promote wound healing. Instead, health care providers had taken a more passive approach, closing wounds, keeping them moist and sterile, and allowing nature and antibiotics to take their course. Now, however, recombinant DNA technology is available to produce large quantities of the human growth factors (HGFs) that occur naturally in the body and have a potent stimulating effect on cell migration and cell division, the two processes central to healing.

Growth factors are polypeptides that are secreted by certain cells and can bind to special receptors on the surfaces of cells. When a growth factor molecule binds to a receptor, it sends a biochemical signal into the cell's interior in ways that can stimulate or inhibit cell growth or movement.

The fact that babies operated on in utero are born totally without scars suggests that the fetus, in response to being cut, produces entirely new tissue. Growth factors apparently play a different role in wound healing in the unborn than in those who have left the womb. The ultimate in wound healing will be to apply what has been learned about fetal healing to those in the world outside the womb.[28] This may not be a clinical reality until 2005 or later, however.

In the meanwhile, researchers of today have found that treatment of infected wounds with fibroblast growth factor (FGF) improves the rate of wound closure. Recent studies indicated that conventional therapeutic agents are toxic to the cells responsible for healing and, thus, retard the process.[29] Treatment with FGF, then, may become the lead technology for wound healing until the results of further fetal research are available.

Interleukins

Medical researchers are currently investigating interleukins, which are natural components of the immune system. Although they themselves are not toxic to the patient, they stimulate the immune system to fight disease. For example, certain leprosy patients are known to benefit from multidrug therapy (i.e., the administration of dapsone, rifampicin, and clofazamine), although several years of treatment are required. In contrast, experiments have shown that the administration of interleukin-2 (IL-2) twice daily for 8 days gives results equivalent to those of one regimen of multidrug therapy. It is now hoped that the same results will ensue in the treatment of tuberculosis, fungal infections, herpes simplex virus, cytomegalovirus, varicella-zoster virus, as well as human immunodeficiency virus (HIV). It is expected that IL-2 will also be beneficial in the treatment of infections with parasites such as *Leishmania*, *Pneumocystis*, and *Toxoplasma*.[30] IL-2 has been used for several years as an experimental cancer treatment, and its clinical use is foreseeable.

Genetic Therapies

Once thought of as a pipe dream, gene therapy will engender a new direction in medicine. The potential applications of this type of therapy are legion; for example, its use is already being discussed in the treatment of heart disease, diabetes, cancer, and liver disease. Studies are currently being conducted in a variety of areas (Table 1). In time, gene therapy will make it possible to correct genetic deficiencies not only in utero, but also in adulthood.[31]

Routine clinical use of single-gene therapies is approaching, but for several years that use will be confined to major hospitals. Fortunately, the basic skills for the use of such complex biotechnologies are already in place in many of today's clinical laboratories. Steps are now under way, by a number of hospital and laboratory supply companies, to develop the devices, supplies, and additional training required for on-site single-gene therapies.[32]

There is a distinct probability that therapies for multigene disorders will have evolved by the end of the century. They are likely, however, to remain as experimental rarities in the face of the extraordinary complexities inherent in such therapies.

The marketplace for today's new wonders (e.g., the colony-stimulating factors, interleukins, growth factors, and single-gene therapies) will

Table 1. Gene Therapy

Using Viruses	Delivery	Target Diseases
Retroviruses	E	Cancer, SCID, muscular dystrophy, hypercholesterolemia
	I	Cystic fibrosis, cancer, AIDS, genetic blindness
Adenoviruses	I	Cystic fibrosis, cancer, emphysema, muscular dystrophy
Using Other Techniques		
Bound DNA	I	Hypercholesterol-aemia, hepatitis B, haemophilia
Naked DNA	I	Muscular dystrophy, human growth hormone deficiency, flu, AIDS
Physical or	E	Haemophilia, anaemia
Chemical means	I	N/A

E = Ex vivo; I = In vivo.
Source: The Economist; *MedPRO Month*

grow rapidly through the rest of this century. The therapies resulting from these new technologies, along with emphasis on wellness and prevention, will cause today's miracles to pale in the marketplace by 2020, however.

Tomorrow's Therapeutics

If, in thinking of the future, it was necessary to consider only the biotechnologies that have already been discussed, foresight would be a rigorous intellectual exercise—but readily doable by slightly exponential extrapolations to near this century's end. These are only a hint of tomorrow's technologies, however.

Individualized Therapies

Although introduced in this century, individualized therapy may be thought of as a technology of tomorrow. Described as a patient-specific modality of medical biotherapy, adoptive therapy is a very promising candidate to replace the present conventional (and relatively ineffective) cancer triumvirate of surgery, radiation, and chemotherapy. This individualized chemotherapy consists of the following steps:

1. Removal of a small nodule of a patient's tumor (which is biologically unique to that patient);
2. Incubation of the tumor in the laboratory with IL-2;
3. Death of the tumor cells during this "out-of-body" incubation and rapid growth of the patient's tumor-infiltrating lymphocytes (TILs);
4. Addition of more IL-2 to the tailor-made drug and return to the patient's body to complete the treatment.

This new individualized therapy has been under development at the National Cancer Institute (NCI) for several years and has been used successfully on patients. A number of full-scale clinical trials are underway or scheduled.

The Food and Drug Administration (FDA) has been pondering possible regulatory actions as individualized therapy moves in the direction of becoming an accepted medical practice. Historically, the FDA has refrained from regulating either surgeons and their surgeries or the clinical practice of medicine (except indirectly through the system of diagnosis-related groups). Individualized therapy, having much in common with clinical practice, may thus escape regulation, but probably not without debate since it includes the design and manufacture of customized substances for therapeutic use.[33]

Genetic Vaccines

Producing an immune reaction against a particular foreign protein by vaccination ordinarily requires first a purification of that protein and then the injection of the protein or some altered form of it into the body to stimulate the production of antibodies. A recently reported shortcut introduces the gene for the antibody directly into an animal where the gene expresses the required antibody in vivo. The delivery mechanism for this vaccination by gene is a biological/ballistic or biolistic device. This tiny hand-held "shotgun" fires tiny gold microspheres coated with the genetic material directly into the host cells.[34] As a successful vaccine removes the need for treatment, the development of vaccines for diseases such as AIDS, cancer, influenza, and the common cold not only would sharply reduce the number of hospital admissions and office calls, but also would alter the types of therapies most often needed.

Monoclonal Antibodies—At Last

After their introduction more than a decade ago, monoclonal antibodies (MABs) failed to live up to their press. This arose primarily from an overenthusiastic media and the lack of detailed knowledge as to the behavior of organic molecules. Time is curing this problem.

As but one of many current examples, the National Cancer Institute has found in initial experiments that a mouse MAB linked to a radioisotope is effective in treating adult T-cell leukemia. The mouse MAB used is an anti-Tac (T cell–activated) MAB that blocks the IL-2 receptor on the T cell. This action prevents the growth factor IL-2, which the T cell needs to stay alive and divide, from locking onto the T cell. The attached isotope is an extra "gun" to ensure destruction of those leukemic cells that are too far gone at the time of therapy for the MAB alone to be effective.[35]

Developments in the diagnostic use of MABs will be equally impressive. Because an MAB can be made to seek out and attach itself to any pathogen, an MAB can be used to confirm the identity of any suspected pathogen (e.g., a specific virus or cancer cell). If the suspected pathogen is indeed present, attaching a radionucleotide to the MAB makes it possible to determine the location of the pathogen as well. Although it may appear at first that this technique will become the primary diagnostic tool, such a development is unlikely. In many cases, PCR and LCR can identify the pathogen from a blood sample so that there is no need to inject an MAB; in other cases, perhaps in the period 1995 to 2000, the new sophisticated imagers (e.g., MRI spectroscopy for biopsies) will be able to provide accurate diagnoses.

The new wave of MAB use in therapeutics should be cresting between 1995 and 2000. Even though today's health care providers in the trenches perceive MABs as the very latest in treatment, they will eventually perceive antisense technologies, the use of transcription factors to manipulate intermolecular information and to correct misinformation transfer, and several whole new classes of therapeutics currently under investigation as more effective than MABs in the treatment of many diseases. Biosensors, polymerase chain reactions, and magnetic resonance spectroscopy will be found more effective diagnostically than are MABs in many cases. It is likely, however, that MAB technology will find many long-term niches.

Antisense Technology†

The first step in the normal chain of events in the cell, as it makes the proteins essential for life, is the transcription of the information from the double-stranded DNA onto messenger RNA for subsequent handling. In the view of a decade or so ago, to encourage any other course made no sense. Going against this "sense," antisense technology uses only a single strand of DNA to block the transcription of information to RNA and, thus, the transfer of information. This technology makes its own kind of sense in that it prevents defective genes from expressing themselves as, for example, inherited diseases, some forms of cancer, and many infectious diseases. The first human trials are scheduled for 1992 in the treatment of chronic myelogenous leukemia.[36] The advocates of this designer drug technology see a new era of DNA-based drug design in which many diseases will be effectively treated by the antisense approach to therapeutics.

Transcription Factors

The information contained in genes must be suitably transcribed before cell mechanisms can use it to express (make) molecules to the genetic blueprint. The process by which the genetic information contained in the gene produces a complementary sequence of bases in an RNA chain is called transcription. Transcription factors preside over the information flow. It has been conjectured that there are upwards of 10,000 different transcription factors. Approximately 10% of the

---

† *Sections marked with † are derived substantially from S.N. Davidson, "System 2020 AD," St. Joseph Health System, Orange, California (publication pending). Used with permission.*

entire human genome is dedicated to genes that express these transcription factors.

Like antisense compounds, transcription factors are concerned with the transfer of information. Disease, besides arising from defects that are molecular in nature, are also a result of improperly processed information. Therefore, this very vital process of transcription may turn out to be one of the most important challenges for the rest of this century and the beginning of the next. It could be a way of making genetic therapies both safer and more effective. In that sense, it will be the second generation of genetic therapeutic technologies, probably appearing between 2010 and 2020.

The Enediynes

Ever since the mid-1960s, the literature of chemistry has carried papers about a class of DNA-cleaving molecules known as enediynes. The rational design of these molecules and their biological actions have attracted the interest of those in the medical sciences, because some relatively simple enediynes have been designed, synthesized, and characterized so as to mimic the actions of the more complex, naturally occurring enediyne anticancer antibiotics, such as dynemicin A.

When activated, enediynes, these synthetic molecules damage DNA, both in vivo and in vitro, and display potent and selective anticancer activity.

When activated, these synthetic molecules damage DNA, both in vivo and in vitro, and display potent and selective anticancer activity. These compounds "may be modulated to a fine degree through structural changes that take advantage of chemical principles that capitalize on differences between normal and tumor cells."[37] They are far more potent than anticancer agents such as cisplatin, doxorubicin, vinblastine, and bleomycin. They are also more potent than the highly promising anticancer agent, taxol. A review of the literature on these compounds suggests that they have as much future promise from today's perspective as the colony-stimulating factors, interleukins, and human growth factors had during the late 1980s.

Molecular Dynamics

All of the biodiagnostics, biodiagnostic devices, and biotherapeutics involve biochemical reactions that occur at incredible speed. For example, several million new hemoglobin molecules are manufactured in the bone marrow each second. A central problem in the study of these reactions has been the development of tools to follow these reactions on a real time basis. Although various laser and MRS techniques have been helpful, the chief tool in the study of molecular dynamics is the computer. It has the power not only to record the fastest of reactions, but also to predict reactions.

"The ability to record and predict reactions, which only a few years ago would have been thought to belong in some episode of Star Trek in the twenty-third century, will probably be one of the leading technologies of the twenty-first century."

The ability to record and predict reactions, which only a few years ago would have been thought to belong in some episode of Star Trek in the twenty-third century, will probably be one of the leading technologies of the twenty-first century.[38] New drugs will be designed by means of this technique, rather than through the research laboratory. With this technology, it will be possible to navigate in the space around a pathogen, locate appropriate docking sites for a to-be-designed drug, and deposit a killer cell or toxin in the pathogen.

Pharmaceuticals as Information

There are three principal approaches to the design and development of new generations of therapeutics. In the first, research focuses on the genetic code and the design of therapeutics to block the transmission of deleterious information from genetic sources, such as that encountered in oncogenes. A second class of drugs will be developed to block cell receptors so as to ward off viruses that transmit harmful materials into cells or immune cells that may cause excessive inflammatory reactions. Finally, some researchers will be designing molecules to "interfere with the signalling pathways inside the cells that lead to the uncontrolled growth of cancer, or to inflammation, cystic fibrosis, and other diseases."[39]

Because disease and the treatment thereof are direct results of the successful transmission or blocking of the transmission of information (not just data), it should be useful, in contemplating the future, to think of pharmaceuticals as packets of information for the treatment of disease and of pharmaceutical companies as participants in the information business. This concept should not be restricted solely to drugs. Highly important will be the information needs of the prescribers of the drugs and the medical science laboratories as they formulate drugs for local use from supplies furnished by pharmaceutical companies. The information needs for therapeutic drug monitoring will accelerate as therapeutic protocols become more complex.

> **"Think of pharmaceuticals as packets of information for the treatment of disease and of pharmaceutical companies as participants in the information business."**

Interim Technologies†

A term frequently used in discussing devices for therapy is "halfway technology." For example, the iron lung was hailed as a miracle therapy for polio patients in the 1930s, but it was in reality a halfway technology in the march to the polio vaccines of the 1950s. Similarly, open surgery to remove the gallbladder was a halfway technology for the treatment of gallstones compared to the use of laparoscopy, which, in turn, will become a halfway technology when researchers devise an effective method of dissolving the stones in vivo.

One evolving halfway technology has the potential for filling a niche in health care that no other technology has so far been able to fill. It is a

† *Sections marked with † are derived substantially from S.N. Davidson, "System 2020 AD," St. Joseph Health System, Orange, California (publication pending). Used with permission.*

palliative treatment for hundreds of diseases that are or will become definitively diagnosable, but for which effective therapeutics may not emerge from the research pipeline for several years. This treatment's generic name is therapeutic plasmapheresis. Fundamentally, it is an out-of-body separation process used to remove undesirable entities from the blood. Its most widely recognized use is kidney dialysis.

In the most common currently used version of therapeutic plasmapheresis, MABs that have been designed to bind to specific substances in the blood are firmly attached to tiny beads. The beads are then tightly packed into a cylindrical column, where they form a porous media through which the patient's blood is passed. The MABs lock on to and hold the undesirable components, leaving the cleansed blood to flow through the column for return to the patient.

In 1987, the first FDA approval for therapeutic plasmapheresis was granted for the treatment of idiopathic thrombocytopenic purpura. Today, the list of diseases experimentally treatable by this technology includes more than 75 diseases and is increasing daily. In addition, clinical trials of devices intended to isolate cancer cells from the patient's marrow before reinfusion in an autologous bone marrow transplantation are beginning.[40]

As in many new technologies, "turf" questions arise. Who will operate these devices, and where? According to one executive, "it might be easier for clinical laboratory personnel to develop the skills for ex vivo therapeutics than for physicians or nurses to do it themselves."[41] Furthermore, health care providers may more readily accept ex vivo cell therapies if they are promoted by and administered under the guidance of certified laboratory technicians.

Any disease with symptoms that come from undesirable substances in the blood can theoretically be treated by this blood-washing technique. In view of the expenditures associated with treating just one of them (i.e., treatment of renal disease through kidney dialysis), however, it is not feasible to consider treating hundreds of different diseases by means of this technology. Further dramatic advances in new therapeutics will probably make this expensive halfway technology unnecessary.

Community Clinical Trials

The American Cancer Society has stated that "about 52% of all cancer patients with potentially life-threatening cancers are being cured. Broader participation in clinical trials could hike that to 75% by the year 2000; yet today not even 2% of Americans with cancer are in trials."[42] This 2% figure could easily be enlarged. Patients with acute nonlymphatic leukemia; melanoma; or cancer of the breast, stomach, colon, rectum, lung, prostate, or bladder can be enrolled in an NCI "high-priority" trial in their own communities. Information about NCI-sponsored clinical trials can be obtained merely by dialing 1–800–4–CANCER.

The technology is ready for community trials. Are physicians ready? In reality, for years they have selected patients in a de facto and informal form of clinical trials by prescribing drugs for off-label uses. Many third-party payers (e.g., Blue Cross and Blue Shield) have acknowledged this practice.[43] Some community physicians will be reluctant to put their patients into formal clinical trials, however. The extra paperwork and monitoring needed to comply with strict clinical trial protocols would consume the time of busy practitioners who want to treat patients, not do paperwork.

"The technology is ready for community trials. Are physicians ready? In reality, for years they have selected patients in a de facto and information form of clinical trials by prescribing drugs for off-label uses."

Even so, what is true now for cancer will be true for most diseases during the 1990s. Starting with community trials for AIDS patients in the 1980s, the trend toward clinical trials at the community level has been both apparent and inevitable. Arthritis and heart disease activists have taken up the fight for such trials. Perhaps we are more ready than we know. As Michael McDonald points out in his paper, we will have a much more supportive infrastructure for this type of community trial. Tomorrow's medical sciences laboratory, with its new high technologies and capabilities, will be able to support local health care facilities and practitioners in their roles in what will be a long-lasting and widespread network of ongoing clinical trials.

The Medical Science Laboratory

Clearly, advances in the new sciences will have an important impact on the clinical laboratory. As noted by the American Hospital Association (AHA),

> The new technology makes diagnosis possible at the genotypic level, which provides a far more definitive and reliable diagnostic tool. These new approaches have the potential to change the practice of laboratory medicine in the same way in which computed tomography and magnetic resonance imaging altered the practice of radiology.[44]

New perceptions of clinical laboratory functions are implicit in modified standards recently released by the Joint Commission on Accreditation of Healthcare Organizations. These new standards state, "Qualified doctoral-level scientists may now become lab directors in accredited institutions." In outlining new eligibility standards, the Joint Commission recommended that the laboratory directors should be PhDs qualified "by virtue of documented training, expertise and experience to assume professional, scientific, consultative, organizational, and educational responsibilities for the facilities and for the services rendered."[45]

Tomorrow's medical science laboratory will have a very broad scientific and communications base. It is likely to evolve into

- A center for the interpretation and integration of routine diagnostic technologies in a new era of increasing certainty of diagnosis;
- A technical and administrative support center for local participation in clinical trials of life-saving therapeutics;
- An information and management center for data inputs from biosensors and other diagnostic technologies used at a wide variety of sites (e.g., bedside, wellness centers, homes, diagnostic centers, and physician offices);

- A medical science department that manages and integrates the present clinical laboratory and pharmacy functions of the community health center in order to support the concept of
  1) An apothecary for the formulation of new individualized biotherapies;
  2) A center for the management of therapeutic drug monitoring needed in conjunction with both local experimental clinical trials and the routine use of the new generations of biotherapeutics.

SURGERY

Improved, less invasive surgeries and pharmaceuticals are replacing conventional open surgical procedures at an ever-increasing rate. For example, transurethral prostatectomy has already replaced most of the prior highly invasive open surgeries to treat benign prostatic hyperplasia. Other endoscopic technologies, such as transurethral ultrasound-guided laser-induced prostatectomy and transurethral microwave thermotherapy, that are being developed are even less invasive than is transurethral prostatectomy.[46,47] Many patients with this condition are refusing surgery, however, and are taking a wait-and-see stance in hopes of being treated with one of the drugs about to be approved for the treatment of benign prostatic hyperplasia. Thus, benign prostatic hyperplasia is a quintessential model for the transitions of many therapies from conventional surgeries, to endoscopic procedures, to treatment by new biopharmaceuticals.

> **"Most open surgeries still being performed in 2020 AD will be endoscopic in nature."**

Most open surgeries still being performed in 2020 AD will be endoscopic in nature. They will combine the dexterity and judgment of a skilled operator; the imaging, data processing, and analytical abilities of the computer; a new generation of robotics; and a three-dimensional intracorporeal navigation system in a suite somewhat resembling today's catheterization laboratory. The facilities are likely to be located in outpatient clinics, community hospitals, or regional centers, depending on the complexity and frequency of each procedure. During the intervening years, the development of new skills by interventionists will be of primary importance.

Tomorrow's Diseases

Many of tomorrow's diseases will result from the identification of "new" ills that have been hidden within an already identified disease with but one name. Since the initial recognition of hepatitis, for example, no fewer than five variants have been identified. Other diseases will be "imported." Among such diseases are new forms of drug-resistant tuberculosis, first noted as a threat in 1991; New York City has reported a doubling of the incidence of this disease since the mid-1980s.[48]

The growing number of the homeless and HIV-infected people, both of whom are immune-suppressed and living in overcrowded, unclean surroundings, provide an ideal environment for the proliferation of tuberculosis. This highly contagious infection with *Mycobacterium tuberculosis* is already showing up in prisons and hospitals across the United States.[49]

A potential severe ethical problem may lie in the announcement of the Health Resources and Services Administration that it plans to use its Hansen's Disease Center to house people "with drug-resistant tuberculosis who are reluctant to take their medication" and are ordered by state and local courts to be detained "so they no longer are a public health threat."[50] If Society decides that this is a justifiable exercise of the right of the many over the right of the few, what, then, about people with AIDS or the many other heretofore rare (for the Western affluent societies) diseases, such as Hantan fever, Lassa fever, Seoul virus, Chagas disease, and dengue fever, that are likely to arrive with waves of immigration? Happily, the capability for rapid and early diagnoses for these diseases will soon be available to the clinical laboratory in the form of the PCR and LCR technologies.

Tomorrow's Physician

The physician community is beleaguered. It faces pressures for change in physician practice styles from well-informed and sometimes litigious patients and patient activist groups; third-party payers, both government and private; legislative actions; the ethical community; and health care facilities. These pressures have a common basic source: the need to make choices from the cornucopia of new technologies that are becoming available for the prediction, prevention, diagnosis, and treatment of disease. Physicians have a vast amount of knowledge in their specialty that must be readily available to apply to the problems of the patients who seek care from them. The application of this knowledge is, by itself, a full-time job with little room for the study of new developments and directions in the sciences underlying their professions.

Making change more difficult for physicians is their limited access to the biomedical advances in either academia or industry. In the words of Cynthia Schmeichel, "There is still a language barrier between the molecular biologist and the physician . . . most often, the rank-and-file practitioners lack adequate information buttressed by peer-validated clinical experience."[51] This means that the physician must rely on others for visions of the future.

"The physician must rely on others for visions of the future."

According to an old anecdote, Sir William Osler said of diagnosis that "more errors are made from not looking than from not knowing." In its time, this was a wise statement. In the present era of information overload and automated looking devices, however, more errors are made from not knowing than from not looking. The tools to look are easily accessible, and the available knowledge base exceeds the capacities of most minds. The myth of the all-knowing physician-scientist must, in an increasingly well-informed society, be abandoned.[52]

Today's scientists train long and hard in the academic realm to complete the required education. The struggle of the scientist is to acquire a philosophical and practical basis for future work. The scientist must deal with the unknown; the physician applies what is known. Recognizing this, medical schools are undertaking measures to ensure that their medical students are taught by tenured PhDs in science rather than professors of medicine. An increasing number of them insist that computer literacy is a must for graduates. During the coming two decades or so, while a new "physician" evolves to meet tomorrow's needs, today's practitioners need to participate more directly in the clinical investigation network. The integration of the community physician into the information network on molecular medicine will be a syncronicity of major importance when coupled with a significant increase of clinical trials at the community level.

What will the twenty-first century physician become? One alternative was suggested in 1976 by Jerrold Maxmen, who described the future replacement for today's physician as a "medic."[53] This person would be a graduate of a 4–year college with an academic background that would be suitable for a first-year student at today's medical college. An empathy for people would also be encouraged. After that would come 12 to 18 months of intensive training in a medical school of tomorrow, followed by assumption of the leadership of patient-centered health care teams with appropriate support from specialist scientists.

However logical Maxmen's detailed rationalizations may appear, it seems unlikely that society will accept such a future. First, our medical traditions are deeply rooted in our society. Second, Maxmen's "medic" is already here and at work under the aliases of nurse-practitioner and assistant physician. Instead of Maxmen's medic, the physician of tomorrow is likely to be a superbly trained physician modeled after today's family practitioner. He or she will be a true generalist who will receive counsel and scientific guidance from highly trained specialists, but who will remain in charge of the patient. Can physicians make this transition?

> To the student who worries that generalist medicine is the practice mode of the past, we would say that quite the opposite is true. Because generalists are skilled in making intuitive connections necessary to analyze the chaotic system called the human being, they will play a central role in our evolving health care system. Generalist care is the practice model of the future. And to the student who questions the scientific validity of primary care medicine, we would say that chaos theory confirms what

we have known all along: general medical practice is also based on science. This scientific basis is neither superior nor inferior to that which underlies specialist medicine—just different. Neither is generalist medicine superior or inferior to specialist medicine; it is instead the balance that Aristotle believed essential for a complete understanding of the world. We would add, to paraphrase Gleick—If you have an eye for pattern, especially pattern that appears on different scales at the same time, if you have a taste for complexity, for jagged edges and sudden leaps, consider a career in primary care medicine. You'd probably enjoy it; we certainly do.[54]

Forces That Will Shape Future Health Care Standards

When diagnosis is a matter of signs, symptoms, and laboratory technologies modulated by the intuitive educated guesses of physicians trained in deductive reasoning, diagnoses are uncertain. Both anecdotal evidence and serious in-depth studies confirm the extent of this uncertainty. Clearly, writing standards for uncertainty is an oxymoron. On the other hand, because certainty of diagnosis implies precisely controlled and relatively specific treatment regimens, it makes standards mandatory. Thus, as certainty in diagnosis and success in therapy increase, so, too, will the need for appropriate standards.

> **"Communication of bioinformation in vivo, ex vivo, and in cogno (the ubiquitous computer) must be a precision effort with equally precise standards."**

In the molecular universe of health and disease, such entities as growth factors and other hormones, enzymes, DNA and RNA molecules and fragments, and genes are packets of information. New age pharmaceuticals will transfer information into the human mind/body to correct information deficiencies or overloads by ingestion, injection, or other means. Communication of bioinformation in vivo, ex vivo, and in cogno (the ubiquitous computer) must be a precision effort with equally precise standards.

Traditionally, drugs have been developed and marketed as end products of a central pharmaceutical company and distributed to patients by hospitals and pharmacies under a physician's order. Most of tomorrow's products, however, will be delivered as precursor "reagents" that become the "drugs" just before their introduction into the patient (i.e., ex vivo) or just after their entrance into the body (i.e., in vivo). Genetic therapies will often have both ex vivo and in vivo segments.

The local manufacture of complex therapeutic molecules will become common. For example, the biosynthesis of such molecular substances as penicillin, vitamin B_{12}, and anticancer alkaloids will take place in bottles that contain the appropriate sets of enzymes and a supply of nutrients. In this context, the bottle acts like a living cell; it is, in a sense, a brewery. The process requires only the correct recipe for the desired product, the proper enzymes, the necessary reagents, a bottle, and a shelf to put the bottle on while the natural process takes place. The one-bottle production of penicillin has already been demonstrated. The enzymes to produce vitamin B_{12} are being developed. Researchers have determined the enzymes necessary for the production of anticancer alkaloids, but have yet to set forth their amino acid sequence and to reverse-engineer the gene to produce those enzymes.[55] The use of community locations for experimental trials, as well as the growth of home health care delivery, will increase the probability of local fabrication of drugs.

One of the few sure things about the future is that it will come before expected. "In 1980 cloning a gene required the efforts of 50 skilled biologists working for eighteen months. Now [1989] the same task takes one single investigator seven days."[56] Thus, 1989 produced the "gene of the week"; however, 1992 seems to be approaching "genes of the day." Furthermore, storing a known gene sequence as digital data is as good as storing it in a vial in a laboratory cabinet. The conversion of genetic information from the binary mode of the computer to the quaternary mode of the four nucleic acids is but a matter of technology, not science, and that technology is already developing.

French Anderson provided a clear view of near-future possibilities when he described the goals of genetic therapy as follows:

- Do all the engineering in advance so a physician can take a vial off the shelf [or out of a digital data bank?] and inject into the patient.
- Be able to insert the gene of choice directly into the tissue that is wanted, into the appropriate place in the chromosome that is wanted, and have it regulated in the way that is wanted.[57]

In the past, the function of the FDA was fairly clear: the regulation of drugs, on the one hand, and medical devices, on the other. Today, work is in progress on approval processes for therapies that involve the concurrent use of drugs and devices, as well as those that involve the manipulation of genes. In fact, the FDA recently approved for the first time a genetically based experimental treatment. As new biotherapies become accepted clinical practices, how will they be regulated and standardized? Will 2020 see the regulation of medical "procedures"? Until now, "medical practice" has not been regulated. In the future, however, many new drug and drug-device combinations will be applied by other than physicians. As such, it is difficult to imagine that they will not be subject to rigorous standards. Moreover, the increasingly global nature of science and medicine may call for new approaches to standard making—governmental, institutional, or private—on an international basis.

"Will 2020 see the regulation of medical 'procedures'?"

Whatever finally becomes the future reality for health care is being forged today in the halls of medical academia, hospital planning departments, medical associations, health centers experimenting with new concepts of patient-centered care, legislatures, courts, government agencies, and the media.

In our best scenario, health care may indeed approach the ideal. The health of our largest patient, the planet Earth, will be a limiting factor, however. The molecular technologies to treat the Earth's human-induced metabolic disorders are at hand or within reach. Human socioeconomic institutions must lead us to the diagnosis and the fair and equitable treatment of that complex of metabolic disorders. Otherwise, whatever scenarios we may write about health care will become moot. In summary, what the new medical sciences can make available for vaccination, diagnosis, prevention, and treatment of disease is limited only by the imagination of the scientist, but their use will be modulated by socioeconomic and ethical considerations.

DISCUSSION SUMMARY

After Stuart Davidson (Director, Center for Technology Assessment, St. Joseph Health System) reviewed his forecasts for medicines and health technology, Robert Levy (President, Wyeth-Ayerst Research) noted that research is by definition uncertain and that there is a gap between what science thinks can be done and what is actually done. The complexity of medical problems is often underestimated. A disease-free planet, according to Levy, is not possible by 2020. There are, for example, likely to be diseases that are as yet unknown. On the positive side, great strides are likely in disease simulation, immunotherapy, and, particularly, gene therapy. In order to deal with a diversity of delivery systems, there will be a diversity of medical education. As a result, there is likely to be a very different breakdown of medical specialties.

In this era of discovery, Charles Leighton (Senior Vice President, Merck Research Laboratories) pointed to the unraveling of DNA as the most important discovery in any field of human history. Some factors in the environment, however, may hinder the translation of even today's biomedical knowledge into practical technological advances in medicine. There is, for example, a crumbling intellectual and scientific infrastructure. Leighton expressed concern that there may be a substantial lack of scientific talent in the United States over the next 30 years. Despite living in this era of scientific discovery, the public seems to know less and less about science. Although technology has improved the quality of human life, the public is unable to grasp the concepts fully.

Leighton also noted that there may well be a search for low-technology solutions to medical problems. There is, for example, a movement to over-the-counter drugs that are safe, have minimal [adverse] effect, and keep patients out of the health care system. Home diagnostic kits are simple, giving yes or no answers to health care questions, and also keep patients out of the health care system. In this vein, patients may turn away from medical specialists and to family practitioners.

Innovation, Leighton continued, may well be judged in the future according to criteria that differ from the criteria used today. The current fascination with technological innovation itself may be redirected toward studies in health economics and social outcomes. Such studies may slow the pace of technological revolution, because they are extremely time consuming. Large patient databases may permit the evaluation of new technology without costly, complicated clinical trials.

According to Dana Ullman (President, Homeopathic Educational Services), the high-technology approach to medicine fails to take into account the "high-natural" approach, particularly the systematic use of natural therapies to promote healing. He said that the different approaches have complementary sets of assumptions. In conventional medicine, symptoms are considered indications that something is "wrong" with the person and must be managed. From the homeopathic perspective, however, symptoms are considered defenses, responses of the organism to stress or infection. Thus, whereas those who practice conventional (allopathic) medicine try to control or suppress the symptoms, homeopaths seek medicinal substances that actually mimic the symptom to help the body heal itself. Both are approaches to stimulating the immune response. Ullman predicted that homeopathy will play a role in the treatment of infectious disease in the future because of this very ability to trigger an immune response. In Europe, homeopathy is an integral part of mainstream medicine today. It seems likely, he noted, to fit into a future approach to health care based on biochemical individuality, systems theory, and even chaos theory.

In homeopathic medicine, Ullman continued, one of the important assumptions is that whatever a substance causes in overdose will stimulate the body's defenses in small doses. Vaccinations and allergy treatments are prime examples. Drug companies, therefore, may find it useful to test the toxicology of substances and determine what symptoms small doses of the substance may be used to treat. This may be a way to speed up the drug approval process, as well as to integrate high-technology and high-natural medicine.

Although the standards of inclusion and exclusion may be different, the work of the U.S. Homeopathic Pharmacopeia complements that of the USP, according to Ullman. The members of the Homeopathic Pharmacopeia Convention include pharmacists, physicians, and consumers. They make recommendations to the FDA as to how they would like to be regulated, and the FDA approves or disapproves those recommendations. Self-policing is also part of their activities. Most practitioners of homeopathy are medical doctors, although other licensed professionals may practice homeopathy. Because homeopathic medicines are over-the-counter drugs, patients also can prescribe for themselves. With written protocols that indicate to consumers when it is appropriate to seek conventional medical care, Ullman declared, the homeopathic system may well complement conventional health care systems in the future and create a more collaborative model.

Several pharmaceutical companies are now entering or considering the possibility of entering the market in homeopathic medicines, as body-mind therapies are coming to the attention of the U.S. public. Because homeopathic medicines are held to a standard of safety, the real questions surround efficacy. The medicines, Ullman argued, are individualized and generic. In Europe, homeopathy is widely accepted, and the European Community has called for a Europe-wide homeopathic pharmacopeia.

Statistics show that people who seek homeopathic care are generally highly educated. Leighton suggested that the education of these patients may not be in the fields of science, however. Ullman responded that, sometimes, patients seek both conventional and alternative care in tandem. Other times, they choose one or the other. People with cancer, for example, may seek homeopathic care when conventional medicine is clearly not working.

In response to a question about whether homeopathy will remain a "traditional" self-care approach or whether there will be a resurgence of homeopathic education, Ullman said that both are likely. Homeopaths encourage the growing emphasis on self-care, although not for chronic or recurring conditions. In Europe, those in the medical profession are more willing to accept differing approaches to medicine than they are in the United States, which may account in part for the broader use of homeopathy. Lasagna added that European and U.S. drug-prescribing habits also differ; for example, the evidence of efficacy is quite different.

Patients focus on the benefit; they do not care what kind of medicine provides the benefit. Grace Powers Monaco (Director, Medical Care Ombudsman Program, Medical Care Management) stressed that people need reputable information systems to make decisions, but such information currently does not exist for the bulk of alternative medicines. Homeopathy is a well-developed discipline, but entrepreneurs who do not understand the remedies of another culture may introduce them to the U.S. market as alternative medicines without proper evaluation. It is essential, concluded Monaco, to fit alternative remedies into the structure for evaluation.

Treatments in the future will be radically different from today's treatments. According to Davidson, advances in technology will become available for clinical use at a geometrically increasing pace. A large part of medical therapy will consist of genetic manipulation. There, however, will be some "orphan" diseases for which such therapy will not be cost-effective. Because genes are information, equivalent to digital information in a computer, and can be used much as a reagent, standards are likely to be necessary for gene use.

Cost containment is another major concern in considerations of individualized therapies. One participant expressed doubt that anyone will risk the capital to develop a new genetic therapy without the high reward associated with benefits for large populations. Levy responded that individualized therapy is not a therapy for one individual, however; gene therapy, for example, may affect millions of patients. Thus, there will be a gene therapy market, although the cost:benefit ratio always will have to be defended.

In response to a question regarding the potential for a merger of drugs and devices, James Boylan (Director, Pharmaceutical Research and

Development, Abbott Laboratories) noted that, for several years now, research has been conducted into combinations of drugs with their plastic or electronic delivery systems. This trend seems to continue. Products are being approved and regulated as systems, so that the FDA is looking at the pieces of the systems under their mandate. More and more, drug-device combinations will appear, and, unless the FDA prepares itself to deal with such combinations effectively, another area of delay in the approval process is likely to be created.

The availability of alternative ways to educate the public is likely to stimulate people to be more informed health care consumers. One family practitioner who attended the conference postulated that he and his colleagues may blend the high and low technologies. Instantaneous computerized information exchange, for example, may become a major component of the practitioner's office. Resources should be online and running, as future physicians all will be comfortable using high technology.

> **"New therapies, particularly the individually tailored medication developed in the laboratory, may lead to combinations of pharmacies and laboratories."**

New therapies, particularly the individually tailored medication developed in the laboratory, may lead to combinations of pharmacies and laboratories. Kenneth Barker (Professor and Head of the Department of Pharmacy Care Systems, Auburn University) commented that there will be substantial changes in the distribution system brought about by such combinations. In addition, conflicts among regulatory authorities may arise as a result of these combinations.

NOTES

1. H. Harley, J. D. Brook, S. A. Rundle, S. Crow, W. Reardon, A. Buckley, P. Harper, D. E. Houseman, and D. Shaw, "Expansion of an Unstable DNA," *Nature* 355(1992):545–546.
2. J. Buxton, P. Shelbourne, J. Davies, T. Van Tongeren, C. Aslanadis, P. de Jong, G. Jansen, M. Anvret, B. Riley, R. Williamson, and K. Johnson, "Detection of an Unstable Fragment of DNA Specific to Individuals with Myotonic Dystrophy," *Nature* 355(1992):547–548.

3. C. Aslanidis, G. Jansen, C. Amemiya, G. Shutler, M. Amemiya, C. Tsilfidis, C. Chen, J. Alleman, N. Wormskamp, M. Vooijs, J. Buxton, K. Johnson, H. Smeets, G. Lennon, A. Carrano, R. Korneluk, B. Wieringa, and P. De Jong, "Cloning of the Essential Myotonic Dystrophy Region and Mapping of the Putative Defect," *Nature* 355(1992):548–561.
4. M. Mahadevan, C. Tsilfidis, L. Sabourin, G. Shutler, C. Amemiya, G. Jansen, C. Neville, M. Narang, J. Barcelo, K. O'Hoy, S. Leblonde, J. Earle-Macdonald, P. De Jong, B. Wieringa, and R. Korneluk, "Myotonic Dystrophy Mutation: An Unstable CTG Repeat in the 3″ Untranslated Region of the Gene," *Science* 255(1992):1253–1255.
5. Y. Fu, A. Pizzuti, R. Fenwick, Jr., J. King, S. Rajnarayan, P. Dunne, J. Dubel, G. Nasser, R. Perot, T. Ashizawa, P. De Jong, B. Wieringa, R. Korneluk, M. Perryman, H. Epstein, and C. Caskey, "An Unstable Triplet Repeat in a Gene Related to Myotonic Dystrophy," *Science* 255(1992):1256–1258.
6. I. Oberle, F. Rousseau, D. Heitz, C. Kretz, D. Devys, A. Hanauer, J. Boue, M. Bertheas, and J. Mandel, "Instability of a 550-Base Pair DNA Segment and Abnormal Methylation in Fragile X Syndrome," *Science* 252(1991):1097.
7. E. Kremer, M. Pritchard, M. Lynch, S. Yu, K. Holman, E. Baker, S. Warren, D. Schlessinger, G. Sutherland, and R. Richards, "Mapping of DNA Instability at the Fragile X to a Trinucleotide Repeat Sequence p(CCG)n," *Science* 252(1991):1711–1714.
8. A. La Spada, E. Wilson, D. Lubahn, A. Harding, and K. Fischbeck, "Androgen Receptor Gene Mutations in X-linked Spinal and Bulbar Muscular Atrophy," *Nature* 352(1991):77–79.
9. Editorial, *Science* 253(1991):382.
10. S. N. Davidson, "The Molecular Nature of Disease," *Technology Assessment Newsletter* 7, no. 3(1991):1.
11. *MedPRO Month* 1(1991):187.
12. D. N. Belliveau, D. Kennedy, R. McKinstry, B. Buchbinder, R. Weiskoff, M. Cohen, J. Veva, T. Brady, and B. Rosen, "Functional Mapping of the Human Visual Cortex by Magnetic Resonance Imaging," *Science* 254(1991):716–719.
13. C. T. W. Moonen, P. Van Zijl, J. Frank, D. LeBihan, and E. Becker, "Functional Magnetic Resonance Imaging in Medicine and Physiology," *Science* 250 (1990):53–60.
14. M. Stehling, R. Turner, and P. Mansfield, "Echo-Planar Imaging: MRI in a Fraction of a Second," *Science* 254(1991):43–49.
15. H. Erlich, *PCR Technology* (New York, Stockton Press, 1989).
16. D. Holzman, "A Tool for All Seasons," *Mosaic* 23, no. 2(1992):2–11.
17. Ibid.
18. J. S. Schultz, "Biosensors," *Scientific American* 265(1991):64–69.
19. *Medical Laboratory Observer* 22, no. 7(1990):32–35.
20. *Research Resources Reporter, NIH* 15, no. 3(1991):13–14.
21. *Clinical Lab Letter* 13(1992):108.
22. S. N. Davidson, "Biosensors," *St. Joseph Health System Center for Technology Assessment Newsletter* 7(1991):3.
23. "The Ultimate Biosensor," *St. Joseph Health System Center for Technology Assessment Newsletter* 8(1992):4.

24. L. Roberts, "Fishing Cuts the Angst in Amniocentesis," *Science* 252(1991):378–379.
25. *Clinical Lab Letter* 12, no. 19(1990):147–148.
26. *Blue Sheet, F-D-C Reports* 34, no. 23(1991):4–5.
27. C. Marwick, "Immune System Boosters Set for FDA Go-Ahead," *New England Journal of Medicine* 265(1991):841–842.
28. P. Skerrett, "Matrix Algebra Heals Life's Wounds," *Science* 252(1991):1066.
29. P. Hayward et al., "Fibroblast Growth Factor Reverses the Bacterial Retardation of Wound Contraction," *American Journal of Surgery* 163, no. 3(1992):288–292.
30. G. Kaplan, Z. Cohn, and K. Smith, "Rational Immunotherapy with Interleukin 2," *Bio/Technology* 10, no. 2(1992):157–162.
31. B. Culliton, "Gene Therapy on the Move," *Nature* 354(1991):429.
32. "Gene Therapy: A New Role for Clinical Labs?" *Clinical Lab Letter* 13, no. 4(1992):25.
33. S. Rosenberg, "Adoptive Immunotherapy for Cancer," *Scientific American* 262, no. 5(1990):62–69.
34. T. De-chu Tang, M. DeVit, and S. Johnson, "Genetic Immunization Is a Simple Method for Eliciting an Immune Response," *Nature* 356(1992):152–154.
35. *Blue Sheet, F-D-C Reports* 35, no. 17(1992):7–8.
36. T. Beardsley, "Making Antisense," *Scientific American* 266, no. 2(1992):107–108.
37. K. C. Nicolaou, W.-M. Dai, S.-C. Tsay, V. Estevez, and W. Wrasidio, "Designed Enediynes: A New Class of DNA-Cleaving Molecules with Potent and Selective Anticancer Activity," *Science* 256(1992):1172.
38. A. Moffat, "Molecular Dynamics and the Modeler's Art," *Mosaic* 22, no. 4(1991):3–11.
39. A. Gibbons, "Biotech's Second Generation," *Science* 256(1992):767.
40. *Clinical Lab Letter* 13, no. 8(1992):59–60.
41. *Clinical Lab Letter* 13, no. 2(1992):11.
42. "Treatments of Last Resort?" *Harvard Health Letter* 17, no. 1(1991):9–12.
43. *Blue Sheet, F-D-C Reports* 33, no. 44(1990):4.
44. J. W. Steiner, "Regionalization of Laboratory Care: A Viable Option for the 21st Century," *Hospital Technology Series* 9, no. 16(1990):16.
45. *Clinical Lab Letter* 12, no. 13(1991):102.
46. *Johns Hopkins Medical Letter* 3, no. 8(1991):1–2.
47. *Health Technology Trends, ECRI* 4, no. 1(1992):5.
48. *Blue Sheet, F-D-C Reports* 34, no. 48(1991):11.
49. *Science* 255(1992):148–149.
50. *Blue Sheet, F-D-C Reports* 35, no. 12(1992):5.
51. C. Schmeichel, "Molecular Medicine: Too Much Too Soon?" *Bio/Technology* 9, no. 11(1991):1063.
52. F. D. Ledley, "The Physician-Scientist's Role in Medical Research and the Mythology of Intellectual Tradition," *Perspectives in Biology and Medicine* 34, no. 3(1992):410–420.

53. J. Maxmen, *The Post-Physician Era* (New York, Wiley Interscience, 1976).
54. H. T. Pruessner et al., "The Scientific Basis of Generalist Medicine," *Academic Medicine* 67(1992):232–235.
55. E. Pennisi, "Bottled Enzymes Make Complex Chemicals," *Science News* 142, no. 10(1992):148.
56. Editorial, American Association for the Advancement of Science *Observer*, November, 1989, p. 5.
57. *Blue Sheet, F-D-C Reports* 35, no. 35(1992):8.

Molecular Nanotechnology and Its Possible Pharmaceutical Implications

by Gregory M. Fahy, Ph.D.
American Red Cross
*Rockville, Maryland**

Sometime in the next 30 years, mankind should acquire an unprecedented ability to grasp, manipulate, and modify individual molecules. This ability may have profound implications for drug standards, drug information, and the nature of drugs themselves. The term *molecular nanotechnology* has been coined to mean the technology of highly versatile and inexpensive molecular fabrication, molecular manipulation, and molecule-level manufacturing. It refers to the nanometer size range, the scale of atoms and molecules, but could be used to create macroscopic structures of precisely defined composition. The key concepts of molecular nanotechnology are that molecules can be machines and that molecular engineers can work with molecules to build desired equipment just as effectively as today's engineers now work with bulk materials. The difference between nanotechnologists and biotechnologists is that the former do not restrict themselves to the biological limitations of the latter, and they are much more ambitious about the kinds of accomplishments that they want to achieve.

Organic chemists have long been able to synthesize complex molecular structures, including drugs, by devising ingenious reagents and by contriving reaction conditions in such a way as to minimize undesired side reactions and maximize their yield. The results obtained depend on the statistics of uncontrolled molecular collisions in solution involving all possible molecular degrees of freedom. Statistically improbable reactions may be slow. More important, solution-based reactions generally lead to unwanted and potentially toxic byproducts. This imprecision of present day chemical synthesis and manufacturing processes is one reason that drug standards are needed. In contrast, molecular nanotechnology would directly and rapidly produce the desired chemical and only the desired chemical, giving yields of virtually 100%. This would be achieved by precisely positioning and bringing together the individual molecules involved in the reaction in such a way as to catalyze the reaction desired and only the reaction desired.

"Molecular nanotechnology would directly and rapidly produce the desired chemical and only the desired chemical, giving yields of virtually 100%."

Pathways to Molecular Nanotechnology

Molecular nanotechnology has many precedents. Enzymes are natural molecular machines that adsorb individual reagent molecules from the surrounding solution and, as a result of precisely orienting them with respect to each other in a protected "nanoenvironment," catalyze reactions in a highly specific manner at very high speeds and under mild reaction conditions. This simple process in biological systems ultimately allows synthesis of structures as diverse as carbon dioxide and hair. In fact, living organisms are naturally existing, fabulously complex systems of molecular nanotechnology. If nature can produce the biochemical capabilities of living cells by accident, molecular engineers should be able to accomplish comparable, but broader, capabilities by design, guided in part by the examples of living systems.

Many industries already make use of enzymes to catalyze desired reactions one molecule at a time. Genetic engineers are producing pharmaceuticals by using naturally occurring enzymes to edit DNA, and the soft drink industry uses enzymes that have been modified to allow them to produce sugar at high rates near 100°C without denaturation. The real promise for the future, however, lies in the development of fully artificial enzymes. Enzymes have already been designed, synthesized, and found to function as designed. Designed enzymes that are found not to function as intended can be modified as many times as necessary until they function as desired. Thus, whether from first principles or from enlightened trial and error, industrially useful artificial enzymes should be forthcoming. More than 10^{100} average-sized synthetic enzymes are possible with the use of nature's 20 amino acids, whereas probably less than 10^{14} enzymes are presently responsible for maintaining the entire biosphere.

But there is nothing to restrict artificial enzymes to only 20 amino acids. There are many useful kinds of chemistry that are not easily promoted by natural amino acids. One particularly versatile method for transcending the biological limits of proteinaceous catalysts has already been demonstrated.[1] It is based on the fact that the genetic code specifies amino acids by the sequence of any one of four nucleic acid bases taken three at a time, with each three-letter base sequence known as a codon. There are 64 such codons in all, but nature uses them to specify only 20 amino acids rather than 64. Recently, it has become possible to create an artificial transfer RNA that can add an unnatural amino acid to a growing polypeptide chain in response to one of the "unused" codons that exist naturally. This could be expanded to an unlimited number of unnatural amino acids, and these unnatural amino acids could contain totally nonbiological catalytic groups or even pre-made machine parts, such as structural support struts, molecular bearings, or the like. In a fully artificial system, the 20 natural amino acids might even be entirely dispensable. Furthermore, it is now possible to insert artificial bases into DNA and RNA, drastically augmenting the prospects for designing catalytically active RNA as well as proteins with unnatural functional groups.[2] The potential for programming the creation of unprecedented chemical catalysts and other molecular tools useful for molecular engineering is thus virtually open-ended.

Yet a ribosomal pathway to molecular nanotechnology is far from the only viable approach. Bulk techniques are now creating useful building blocks for molecular nanotechnology, such as carbon closed-end tubes with walls that are one atom thick (descendants of Buckminsterfullerene). Cryptands or cavitands are being created that pack the catalytic punch of enzymes into nonproteinaceous structures far smaller than natural enzymes. At the same time, the ability of the scanning tunneling microscope not only to image, but also to manipulate individual atoms and molecules is being combined with the biological specificity of antibodies in an attempt to make all-purpose molecular synthesizers similar in concept to the industrial robots that now make automobiles. These present-day efforts are being supplemented by computational chemistry simulations of molecular bearings, molecular planetary gears, and molecular robot arms that would direct molecular factories.

IMPLICATIONS

An important premise of molecular nanotechnology is that the products of this technology should ultimately be readily affordable. This premise is based on the notion that an all-purpose molecular assembler should be able to make copies of itself. Thus, once the first programmable molecular assembler is made, it will not be long before there are as many such assemblers as the market needs.

Designs for computers with molecular data storage and processing elements predict data storage capacities of 1,000 megabytes per cubic micron and data-processing capabilities of 10^{10} operations per second for similar volumes. Translated into a sugar cube-sized personal computer, this molecular computer would store 10^{20} bytes of information and process information at a speed of 10^{20} operations per second. This is 200 billion times the information storage capacity of today's top level personal computer and well over 100 million times the processing speed of today's fastest supercomputers.

Although it is difficult to project how many of the open-ended possibilities suggested by molecular nanotechnology will be realized by the year 2020, several innovations seem worth considering.

Standards

Quality control in the pharmaceutical industry today is necessary due to the imprecision of the manufacturing, purification, and packaging processes and the inability to monitor product quality on a continuous basis. When drugs are made by programmable molecular fabricators and when molecular sensing devices are available, continuous sensing of the near-flawless production process should be possible, both for internal use and for reporting purposes. Problems could be corrected instantly by replacing defective chemical synthesizers with backup copies and discarding the few molecules of mis-synthesized material before any has a chance to leave the factory. Thus, the products reaching the public should conform to standards with virtually exact fidelity. It is also possible that multipurpose drug synthesizers could be on hand in most clinical chemistry and toxicology laboratories and would make on-site de novo synthesis an alternative to obtaining pre-synthesized standards. The barriers to this route could be more political than technical, but the availability of rapid local synthesis could make a life-or-death difference in some cases, such as those involving acute poisoning, for example. Alternatively, and more probably, instruments capable of identifying and quantitating drugs without calibration standards should be feasible.

"Tomorrow's 'smart' pharmaceuticals could be essentially programmable machines with a range of 'sensory,' 'decision-making,' and 'effector' capabilities."

"Smart" Pharmaceuticals

Today's drug is essentially a single molecule with an often sophisticated, but always limited repertoire. Tomorrow's "smart" pharmaceuticals could be essentially programmable machines with a range of "sensory," "decision-making," and "effector" capabilities. They might avoid side effects and allergic reactions by coming in generic, biocompatible housings; becoming active only upon reaching their ultimate destinations; and attaining almost complete specificity of action. They might check for overdosage before becoming active, thus preventing accidental or intentional poisoning. They might have not one chemical action but several, processing targeted invading organisms or malignant cells through a series of chemical reactions that guarantee the death of the target. They might work in concert with three or four "sister" agents that together produce versatility unattainable by one agent alone.

Despite the vast increase in complexity over present-day drugs, such agents can be expected to be totally "pure" and predictable in their behavior. Safety and efficacy may be inherent in the designs of such "drugs," in which case regulatory issues could be simplified rather than complicated.

Drug and Health-Related Information

When every intelligent person can have essentially unlimited data storage and data-processing capability at his or her fingertips, drug information will change dramatically.

"The opportunities for precise tailoring of individual treatment and for preventive medicine, with all the cost savings implied by both, would be revolutionary."

Marked advances in diagnostic agents could have far-reaching consequences. The year 2020 will occur approximately 15 years after the human genome has been completely sequenced. By 2020, great advances in understanding biochemical individuality, which is so important for side effects and proper dose adjustment, will have been made. This may make it possible for the physician to read critical aspects of a patient's phenotype from a noninvasively obtained cell sample (e.g., cheek lining cells) and to inject "smart" diagnostic agents that can be recovered in a drop of saliva some time later and read out to reveal signs of previously undetected, impending disease processes. The opportunities for precise tailoring of individual treatment and for preventive medicine, with all the cost savings implied by both, would be revolutionary.

"Drug information" could come to include the complete matrix of appropriate pharmacological responses to the newly available individuality data. Eventually, this will become so complex and extensive that the physician will be utterly dependent on assistance provided by computer "expert systems" in making decisions. In the long run, particularly if ingestible diagnostic agents and home readout systems become available, the need for physician participation in pharmacological therapy may vanish altogether for those patients with the right equipment available. A major incentive for this decentralization of medical care will be ethical concerns over patient privacy and the use of phenotypic information for unauthorized purposes: these are issues of "drug information" that continue to redefine the term. Relevant compendia should be available on-line to any interested party, particularly those whose software allows them to interface the data with a medical "expert system."

"Drug documentation will come to resemble today's protein structural databases because of the potentially great complexity of 'pharmaceutical agents' that differ from medical devices only in that they are injectable and/or invisible to the naked eye."

Information about "drugs" per se will also change dramatically. Drug documentation will come to resemble today's protein structural databases because of the potentially great complexity of "pharmaceutical agents" that differ from medical devices only in that they are injectable and/or invisible to the naked eye. Indeed, the line between pharmaceuticals and medical devices will become fuzzier and fuzzier. On the other hand, the need to document contraindications, side effects, and complications of use should be considerably reduced.

Conclusion

Clearly, the world of health care technology will be substantially different in 2020 from that of today. The need for pharmaceutical scrutiny by medical practitioners could be even more intense, however, as all aspects of pharmaceutical medicine and the pharmaceutical industry itself continue to change dramatically and at great speed. It can be hoped that molecular nanotechnology, in addition to helping to create these dramatic changes, will also be one of the technologies that helps the practitioners of 2020 stay abreast of and manage these developments.

Additional Information

For additional information on molecular nanotechnology, the reader is referred to the following sources:

Nanosystems: Molecular Machinery, Manufacturing, and Computation
K. Eric Drexler
Philadelphia, John Wiley & Sons, 1992

The Foresight Institute
Box 60775
Palo Alto, CA 94306
(415) 324-2490

Additional references on pathways to nanotechnology are available in: G. M. Fahy, "Short-term and Long-term Possibilities for Interventive Gerontology," *Mt. Sinai J. Med.* 58(1991):328–340.

NOTES

1. C. J. Noren, S. J. Anthony-Cahill, M. C. Griffith, and P. G. Schultz, "A General Method for Site-specific Incorporation of Unnatural Amino Acids into Proteins," *Science* 244(1989):182–188.
2. J. A. Piccirilli, T. Krauch, S. E. Moroney, and S. A. Benner, "Enzymatic Incorporation of a New Base Pair into DNA and RNA Extends the Genetic Alphabet," *Nature* 343(1990):33–43.

5

Regulation and Standards Governing Health Care Technologies Through the Year 2020

by William W. Vodra, J.D., Partner
Arnold & Porter
Washington, D.C.

The U.S. Republic was not five decades old when the regulation of pharmaceuticals began. This experiment did not involve the young federal government, except as the host to a small group of physicians who gathered in 1820 in the chambers of the U.S. Senate to establish the United States Pharmacopeia (USP). The USP was created to establish uniform standards of identity, strength, quality, and purity for medicines, most of which were either imported chemicals or vegetable extracts that had to be compounded locally by a pharmacist or physician for delivery to a patient. The first national laws to establish drug standards took effect in 1848 after the Mexican War, when U.S. troops, affected by malaria, were sold adulterated and misbranded quinine. Congress then required that all imported drugs and medicines be examined for quality, purity, and fitness for use.

There was no domestic drug industry in 1848, but matters changed in the last half of the nineteenth century, and new laws were enacted during the Roosevelt progressive era. One of these was the Federal Food and Drugs Act of 1906, which established the twin concepts of "adulteration" and "misbranding" that remain in the law to this day.

In the 1906 act, Congress also turned to the *United States Pharmacopeia* (*USP*) and the *National Formulary* (*NF*) to establish standards of purity and quality for drugs and made a manufacturer's failure to meet the USP/NF standards a violation of law. This collaboration between law enforcement officials and nongovernment experts who would specify the standards to be enforced was creative—and has proved successful throughout the twentieth century.

Federal regulation of medicines and medical devices can be seen as a continuing series of responses either to health tragedies or to technological changes that were believed to pose substantial risks. In 1937, for example, an anti-infective sulfa product that was put into solution with diethylene glycol for easy administration to children and marketed as Elixir of Sulfanilamide caused more than 100 deaths and the enactment of the Federal Food, Drug, and Cosmetic Act of 1938. This statute specifically provided that "new drugs" had to be reviewed by the federal government for safety before marketing. The Food and Drug Administration (FDA) was assigned this responsibility. Between 1938 and 1962, Congress passed additional drug legislation every year or two, addressing new technologies such as insulin and antibiotics, creating a federal standard for prescription versus over-the-counter drug status, enhancing the FDA's inspection and law enforcement powers, and regulating color additives used in drug manufacturing.

The next radical expansion of the FDA's power occurred in 1962, when news broke of the thalidomide disaster. Less than 4 months after the press stories swept the nation, Congress had enacted legislation to require affirmative FDA approval before a "new drug" could be marketed, to demand evidence of drug effectiveness (based on adequate and well-controlled clinical studies), to regulate intensively the clinical research process involving experimental drugs, to give the FDA control over prescription drug advertising, and to mandate that drugs be produced in accordance with the currently accepted manufacturing practices in the industry.

In 1976, Congress responded to the Dalkon Shield controversy by enacting the Medical Device Amendments, which created the potential for extensive, drug-type regulation for at least those devices that present the greatest risk of harm to patients. That same year, however, Congress effectively stripped the FDA of much of its regulatory power over vitamins, minerals, and dietary supplements, showing that the legislative actions were not always toward more federal control. Notably, many of the vitamins and minerals had gained a large market as "alternative" therapeutics.

In the early 1980s, Congress began its efforts to utilize the Federal Food, Drug, and Cosmetic Act to provide economic incentives for drug research and innovation, as well as for generic marketing of established drugs. These laws, the Orphan Drug Acts and the Drug Price Competition and Patent Term Restoration Act, are still relatively new, but have had profound effects on the pharmaceutical industry.

Although not all these legislative "remedies" were direct responses to the real or perceived "illnesses" that preceded and justified them, their enactments reflected an increasing belief in the public consciousness that those who, for profit, develop and market pharmaceutical and medical devices should be intensively and pervasively regulated to prevent exploitation of patients and health care providers. Even during the "deregulation" heyday of the early 1980s, there was no attempt to dismantle the health and safety functions of the FDA, and the end of that decade saw the FDA embarking on a vigorous new program of visible and tough regulation.

The long and tenacious history of drug regulation in the United States, stretching from 1820 to today, reflects a persistent public belief that some third party must monitor the industry's activities to prevent any exploitation of those who are sick and vulnerable. Until recently, this view was truly Anglo-American, but other nations have moved toward analogous systems in the past 20 years. Accordingly, it appears that there will be no substantial change in the U.S. public's demand for effective regulation in the next quarter century. The techniques and approaches to regulation may evolve remarkably, but the body politic's expectation about the goals of regulation in terms of consumer protection will not radically change.

Current Regulatory Structure

The FDA regulatory structure for drugs and devices relies on five basic concepts, although they appear under a myriad of different names and in a variety of forms to produce a bewilderingly complex system.

First, the regulatory structure relies on specific, publicly defined standards. The fundamental premise is that an objective test be developed, either by the FDA or by an independent standards-setting organization (e.g., the USP or the Underwriters Laboratories) or by the manufacturer itself (through a pre-market approval application submitted to and reviewed by the FDA). Thereafter, the FDA will apply that test to a sample of the product. If the product fails the test, then it is "adulterated" or "misbranded" and subject to legal action. For example, the standards of identity, strength, quality, and purity embodied in the USP monographs are legally enforceable by the FDA. The agency itself promulgates labeling standards (e.g., the over-the-counter drug monographs), product reference standards (e.g., requirements to show the bioequivalence of generic drugs to the pioneer that was tested for safety and efficacy), performance standards for in vitro diagnostics, and emission standards for radiation-emitting devices. Furthermore, many medical devices are subject to national or international standards that are set by the American National Standards Institute (ANSI) and the International Standards Organization (ISO), and can be enforced by the FDA; these include both product-specific (or product class–specific) requirements and horizontal standards applicable to all devices.

Second, pre-market approval is an important part of drug regulation. Whenever a product requires a pre-market approval, the mere appearance of that product in the marketplace without such an approval is grounds for FDA legal action to remove it. In order to gain approval, the sponsor of the product must first submit to the FDA a package of data and information to demonstrate that the product meets the defined FDA requirements (e.g., safety and effectiveness). These requirements may remain general or be particularized, for example, through guidelines on the design of a clinical trial to assess whether a drug is effective in the treatment of angina pectoris. The package of data and information takes different names: for drugs, it is called a New Drug Application (NDA) or Abbreviated New Drug Application (ANDA); for biologics, a Product License Application (PLA) and a related Establishment License Application (ELA); and for medical devices, either a Premarket Approval Application (PMA or PMAA) or a 510(k), named after the relevant section of the statute. The application must demonstrate not only that the product tested in preclinical and clinical trials met the standards, but also that subsequent batches or lots of product will be sufficiently like those that were tested to permit extrapolation of the findings of safety and effectiveness. The FDA has developed elaborate procedures for evaluating these submissions, and the cost and time necessary to go through the review process are chronic sources of industry and public complaint.

Third, in performing a certain task, a person or firm is expected to follow standard operating procedures (SOPs) that are defined by the person or firm, by the FDA, or by a third party. In this process-oriented, rather than product-oriented approach, the focus is on how work is performed or results achieved. The FDA audits the performance of the regulated parties to assess their compliance with the SOPs for the relevant activity. Noncompliance can justify legal action, even though there may be no evidence that the failure to comply with the SOPs actually compromised the safety or efficacy of the product or the integrity of the process. Thus, for example, pharmaceutical companies must process drugs in accordance with "current good manufacturing practices" in the industry. These practices evolve over time, and each firm is expected to keep up with the state of the art. Among the implementing requirements is one that requires a firm to establish written SOPs for everything from complex quality control testing to routine cleaning of equipment; moreover, the firm must then both follow its SOPs and document that it has followed them. Other process-oriented approaches to regulation can be found in the FDA's "good laboratory practices" requirements for

"Process-oriented approaches to regulation can be found in the FDA's 'good laboratory practices' requirements for nonclinical laboratory studies and the 'good clinical practices' requirements applicable to research that involves human subjects."

nonclinical laboratory studies and the "good clinical practices" requirements applicable to research that involves human subjects. Standards for the conduct of in vitro dissolution tests on solid oral dosage pharmaceuticals are set forth in the *United States Pharmacopeia.*

Fourth, regulatory activity involves active FDA oversight of and continuous FDA participation in critical industry decision making. Because it is so labor-intensive, this direct involvement of government in individual private sector choices is reserved for those areas of extreme importance to public safety. The initiation and evolution of clinical trials on experimental drugs and high-risk devices, for example, are strictly monitored through the Investigational New Drug Application (IND) and the Investigational Device Exemption (IDE).

Finally, the regulatory construct that governs the available information regarding drugs and medical devices differentiates between directly regulated parties and others. The FDA controls the labeling and advertising of the regulated products and may exclude anything that is "false or misleading in any particular," as well as information about a product's clinical uses that have not yet received FDA approval. The restrictions, however, affect only what may be *said* about a product *by* the sponsor of that product. In contrast, scientists are free to speak and publish their data and views of new applications of existing products. Moreover, physicians are technically free to *use* the drug or device as their medical judgment deems appropriate, although approved labeling can influence malpractice rules and restrictions on reimbursement from third-party payers.* This government power over the flow of information has been quite controversial. It is in some respects the regulatory control that is most difficult to harmonize with traditional American views on freedom of speech and government noninterference with the practice of medicine.

Certain common threads exist among the diverse detailed requirements to which individual products or groups of products are subject. On an everyday level, it is customary to consider only those rules that apply to the products of particular interest, but the regulatory maze

---

* *The indirect effects on the use of drugs for indications that are not (at least yet) approved by the FDA and, thus, not allowed to be labeled for such use has led to alternative, independent sources of reliable and authoritative information on the appropriate uses of drugs.*

can become quite confusing. Drugs and medical devices, for example, are subject to independent statutory schemes. The Medical Device Amendments of 1976 established a new and logical structure for devices, premised on the gradations of risk among devices that range from bedpans to magnetic resonance imaging (MRI) scanners, from toothbrushes to artificial hips. These amendments recognize that the effectiveness of a device can often be established by means other than clinical trials and give the FDA the power to rely on such alternate tests. They also reserve preclearance for those products where the risks are greatest and utilize general or specific standards to regulate the balance. For most prescription drugs, however, the regulatory scheme has been harmonized into a unitary structure, despite statutory differences; only biologics are now covered by a truly distinct system.

These same concepts keep manifesting themselves in specific regulatory schemes. The fact is, no truly novel alternative concepts for regulatory purposes in the health and safety arena have been discovered. Thus, it is likely that future regulators will return to these concepts and try to tailor one or more of them to specific perceived needs as they arise. It does not follow, of course, that the FDA will be doing all the regulating. As noted earlier, many of the present regulatory controls are actually defined and implemented by third parties or the industry itself, and merely policed by the FDA.

Future of Regulation

An almost continuous process of evolution marks the statutes governing drug and device regulation. Although public health tragedies are fortunately rare, other forces have led Congress to tinker with the Federal Food, Drug, and Cosmetic Act in virtually every session over the past 50 years. Many of these pressures arose quickly and could not have been predicted. For example, the advent of antibiotics, including a new production technology, coincided with the Second World War, and Congress rushed to design a statutory scheme that would ensure an adequate and safe supply of these vital medicines for U.S. troops. Of course, the crisis caused by acquired immunodeficiency syndrome (AIDS) has had a dramatic impact on the research and approval of new drugs. What similar surprises will occur in the next 30 years?

Some trends are more enduring, and these can be used to gauge some of the likely pressures for change in the regulation of drugs and devices.

Social and Economic Factors

Individual Autonomy versus Government Paternalism. The United States was born from a deep distrust of government and a profound belief in the freedom of the individual citizen. De Tocqueville observed in the early nineteenth century that the United States had designed its political structures to prevent efficient and fully effective control by government officials. The tension between libertarianism or free market values, on the one hand, and government protection of its citizens through regulation, on the other hand, permeates U.S. society. It will not go away, even in an area where society generally distrusts the idea of allowing profit-motivated individuals to sell, that is, to the ill and infirm, without some third-party supervision.

Among the current manifestations of this debate are three prominent examples: the abortion debate, the demand for early access to experimental AIDS drugs, and the persistent popularity of alternative therapies despite regulatory and mainline medical skepticism as to their effectiveness. At the legislative level and, even more potently, at the administrative level, these controversies have shaped and modified FDA policies repeatedly. One can speculate on why the AIDS activists have succeeded when the proponents of laetrile did not and whether the FDA's ban on the importation of RU-486 can be reconciled with its "open door" policy on the importation of unapproved and unproved AIDS therapies, for example, but the answer undoubtedly lies in politics, not in science.

The balance between personal freedom and government intervention to protect patients from themselves (and from exploitation) will be repeatedly disturbed in the next 30 years. The explosion of lay access to medical and scientific information will not subside. Just as the public sale of the *Physicians' Desk Reference* in the early 1980s took drug labeling into the hands of the consumer and the Lifetime network brought medical symposia into every cable television subscriber's home later in the decade, the increasing access to computers and on-line medical libraries will facilitate the public's ability to go behind and beyond the personal physician and the FDA scientist. Already, the AIDS community networks have more current information on clinical trials—their design, status, and results—than do most scientific societies. Thus, the monopoly that FDA has maintained over drug information through the regulation of labeling and advertising may become irrelevant to patients.

"The balance between personal freedom and government intervention to protect patients from themselves (and from exploitation) will be repeatedly disturbed in the next 30 years."

When knowledge about alternative therapies increases among the lay public, the demand for access to these therapies will intensify. Again, the AIDS activists have shown the way to press successfully for the availability of new experimental treatments extraordinarily early in the development process. This is not an anomaly, as shown by the outcry over the FDA's recent seizures of vitamin and mineral preparations. An enormous constituency supports open and unfettered sale of these and other alternatives to mainline allopathic medicine. Despite the FDA's efforts to portray its actions as fighting "health fraud," the FDA is limited in how far it can proceed in law enforcement.

The case of l-tryptophan, in which the FDA removed a nonprescription oral preparation of an amino acid from the U.S. market, represents the one recent exception in which the public still seems fully prepared to allow government to protect consumers of nontraditional medicines. This case, however, was marked by clear evidence of a direct and immediate risk to the users of the product. It confirms that the individual autonomy argument has limits and that U.S. citizens want and expect a third party to prevent producers from actually harming (as opposed to arguably defrauding) consumers.

It appears that, in the future, effective protection of the public health will require credible information from a variety of sources so that individuals can make informed decisions about personal choices as consumers and about public policies as citizens. The FDA cannot and should not act as though it can do the "whole job." Commissioner David Kessler, in fact, has made considerable efforts to reach out to other bodies—federal agencies, state governments, professional societies—to support, reinforce, and extend the FDA's mission. To the extent that other entities can legitimately and competently perform functions that ensure the safety, efficacy, and quality of the drugs and devices available to U.S. citizens, there will be opportunities to do so.

Health Care Costs. The U.S. agony over rising health care costs, decreasing health insurance coverage, and our ability to achieve the avowed goal of health protection for all citizens is obvious. It has a major impact on labor-management negotiations, on the international competitiveness of U.S. industry, on the continued viability of many health insurers and care providers, on the federal and state budget deficits, and on the willingness of physicians and others to remain in the health care profession.

Simply put, the politically viable alternatives and the budgetary deficits will preclude a comprehensive and lasting solution to the problem of rising health care costs in the foreseeable future. Accordingly, one should expect a series of pragmatic and narrowly focused steps to address specific problems, while the agony and pressures continue indefinitely at greater or lesser levels of distress.

The lure of drug substitution (i.e., replacing an expensive product with a lower cost one) will continue to attract policy makers. Although the generic drug "scandal" profoundly harmed regulatory efforts to increase generic drug availability in the early 1980s, these efforts will proceed and may expand in several ways. There is already debate about therapeutic substitution, in which a chemically different drug that costs less and is believed to be able to achieve the same therapeutic effect replaces another drug. Formularies and health insurers, including the Health Care Financing Administration, are demanding evidence that newer drugs and devices be more cost-effective than are existing therapies in order to be eligible for reimbursement. The cost-effectiveness requirements may have a major detrimental effect on new biotechnology products that require substantial investments before comparative trials can take place to assess relative benefits over conventional therapies. The story of recombinant alteplase (TPA) in comparison to streptokinase provides an excellent illustration.

Similarly, interest in outcomes research is growing rapidly. A world in which all products must undergo comparative clinical trials that assess relative safety, relative effectiveness, and relative cost per cure is not implausible. A corollary question is, Who would evaluate these results? Presently, authority is scattered among several bodies; it is not obvious that the FDA, or any single federal agency, should make these assessments. Indeed, were such evaluations to be demanded, the drug and device industries would be likely to seek ways of ensuring speedy reviews and independence between those who passed judgment on the data and those who made purchase or reimbursement decisions based on those judgments. Today, a recurring problem for manufacturers of new therapies is the reluctance of those responsible for budgets to agree to pay for the therapies; thus, actual clinical utilization (and commercial success) can lag months or years behind FDA approval for marketing.

In a similar fashion, it can be predicted that efforts to restrain health care costs will focus more intensively on drug and device utilization. The emerging technologies that will allow each patient's medical history to be encoded on a wallet-sized card and simultaneously tracked and evaluated by insurers and the government will also enable more advanced monitoring of physicians and pharmacists. To be effective, however, standards must be developed and codified to delineate between clearly inappropriate prescribing practices or device utilization and that which is within the legitimate discretion of the physician. Clearly, the medical community will want these standards established by someone other than those who pay the bills in order to ensure that clinical concerns, not economic pressures, inform the judgments.

Another approach to drug utilization is to exclude categorically certain types of drugs or devices (e.g., over-the-counter medications and oral contraceptives, for which providers are commonly not reimbursed now) or to give preferences to some types of therapies over others. This latter idea, if adopted in conjunction with wellness and other preventive care programs, may encourage the use of vitamins, minerals, and so-called nutriceuticals.

Finally, the effort to control health care costs will predictably focus on "unnecessary" costs in the system. For drugs and devices, the most controversial costs involve advertising, promotion, and medical education underwritten by the pharmaceutical industry. The past 2 years have witnessed the largest assault on industry practices in these areas since Senator Kefauver's heyday. Although the FDA originally seemed to want to assume total responsibility for regulating drug firms' activities in medical education and communications, it has recently indicated a willingness to "delegate" tasks to third parties, such as the American College for Continuing Medical Education (ACCME). Again, as technology erodes the effective government monopoly over drug information, the justifications increase for having those outside the FDA take over standards-setting and monitoring duties.

"As technology erodes the effective government monopoly over drug information, the justifications increase for having those outside the FDA take over standards-setting and monitoring duties."

International Markets and Harmonization. The globalization of the economy needs little description. Pharmaceuticals and medical devices uniquely benefit from a global economy. The potential commercial market is limited only by the extent of the disease or disorder being treated, as the safety and effectiveness of drugs and devices are not significantly dependent on racial, ethnic, or cultural differences. The costs of production and transportation pale in comparison to the investment in research and development needed to bring a discovery to the market. Even in the area of production, there are enormous economies of scale that underline the value of a world market. Thus, the existing multinational firms are increasingly interested in the harmonization of regulatory requirements.

There are limits, however, on the speed at which a truly international market can be created. Differences in medical cultures are real; health care insurance schemes and national levels of expenditure on health vary widely; and most nations eschew free market pricing, at least for pharmaceuticals. Moreover, for reasons of politics as well as bureaucratic self-preservation, government agencies will be slow to give up the authority that they have over drugs and devices. Regional frameworks are likely to develop first, as is being seen in the European Community, and may develop under the new North American Free Trade Agreement.

The pharmaceutical industry clearly has a larger stake in harmonization than do national regulatory and political authorities, and the industry will be eager to move more quickly. For-profit manufacturers, acting alone or collectively, cannot be perceived as usurping the regulatory processes. In this environment, third parties have an opportunity to take a lead in accelerating harmonization. For example, efforts are already underway among the pharmacopeias of the United States, Europe, and Japan to consider the harmonization of chemical standards and specifications in active and inactive ingredients in drugs. Likewise, ANSI for the United States, CEN for Europe, and ISO are working to develop and harmonize multinational standards for medical devices.

Changes in the Economics of the Drug and Device Industries. Two special forces at play within the drug and device industries will have their own impacts on the future of regulation: entry costs and excess capacity.

The entry costs for new products and new firms are rising. Apart from any inflation in the price of preclinical or clinical research, drug discovery is becoming more expensive because of the commercial pressures that new products be safer, more effective, and/or more cost-effective than are existing products. The days when it is possible simply to provide an alternate, 16th beta-blocker or 22nd nonsteroidal anti-inflammatory are rapidly disappearing. Similarly, the costs of introducing a new product to the marketplace are increasing, because additional comparative studies must be done, third-party payers must be "sold" on the product, and the medical community must be canvassed rapidly and thoroughly to ensure that the rate of commercial acceptance is swift.

The new importance of the rate at which a product is adopted in clinical practice results from the shortened effective market life of the product, caused both by earlier and deeper penetration of generics at the end of a product's legal patent life and by the risk that an even "safer, more effective, and/or more cost-effective" competitor will appear before the patent expires. Commercial acceptance, in turn, depends on the size and success of the marketing and sales organization. All these factors require ever-increasing capital commitments to sustain the research and development, marketing, and related structures. They also require blockbuster drugs for continued survival; an unsuccessful drug or even a great drug that is useful only for a small market cannot provide the necessary cash flow.

Entry costs may also be increasing for medical devices. Recent amendments to the U.S. device laws, as well as possible reorganizations and policy changes at the FDA, will raise the preapproval and postapproval costs of marketing sophisticated devices. Unlike the pharmaceutical industry, the device industry is marked by small and medium-sized firms that are extremely entrepreneurial in character and for which even modest absolute increases in entry costs can be enormously burdensome.

There has been and remains excess capacity, especially in the pharmaceutical industry. The spate of mergers, joint ventures, and other consolidations among drug manufacturers (e.g., SmithKline and Beecham, Bristol-Myers and Squibb, Genentech and Hoffmann-LaRoche) reflects the disparity between the resources for marketing new products and the number of new products to market.

The effects that these long-term trends may have on drug regulation are varied. The need for rapid commercial acceptance of a product once it has completed the research and development process will increase the demands for an efficient regulatory review process. (Indeed, the recent reports of an agreement between the research-based pharmaceutical industry, the FDA, and Congress for a user fee on NDAs, the proceeds of which would be committed to augmenting the FDA's review capacity and shortening the review period, are evidence of the industry's need for a better FDA.) It would be consistent with this need to allow third parties to take on the portions of the review process that they could do faster or with wider (i.e., international) effect. Thus, the use of nongovernmental organizations to review the chemistry portions of an NDA and establish an international monograph is not beyond consideration.

At the same time, a reduction in the number of companies to be regulated reduces the need for broadly applicable standards. Thus, because there are only two commercial aircraft manufacturers in the United States, the ways in which the Federal Aviation Administration can efficiently carry out its duties are different from the ways that the Federal Deposit Insurance Corporation, which regulates thousands of banks, must use.

"A reduction in the number of companies to be regulated reduces the need for broadly applicable standards."

Technological Factors

Two of the important social and economic trends that have been discussed are technology-driven. First, computers and on-line information services are greatly expanding the lay person's ability to acquire information independently of the government and the personal physician. Second, encoding health information about a patient on a small card and linking health care providers and insurers by computer networks enable utilization review on much wider planes than ever before possible. There are other important technological factors as well.

Refinement and Personalization of Health Risks. Genetic testing is making it possible to identify persons susceptible to certain hereditary diseases. The mapping of the human genome and increased knowledge of the genetic basis of disease may make it possible to define for an individual early in life his or her risk for a wide variety of medical problems. This information may permit earlier intervention and true preventive medicine; it also allows for patient choice. More ominous, it creates the opportunity for insurers to distribute risk on a much more predictable basis. Because the insurance principle of pooling risks suggests stratification and premiums commensurate with risks, it is conceivable that high-risk patients would be excluded from any reasonably priced insurance coverage.

The implications for drug regulation are substantial. First, political pressures may prevent utilization of genetic risk typing, thereby affecting the development of diagnostic products. Second, the extent to which high-risk patients are excluded from coverage would alter the commercial potential for therapies for them and, correspondingly, the need to adjust the regulatory process to encourage the development of newly orphaned products. Third, the prospect for early intervention and preventive care will raise issues of defining and measuring long-term safety and effectiveness.

Personalized Therapies. Already in development are products that literally would take cells or tissue from a patient, modify or proliferate them, and return them to that patient. In other words, there is no mass-produced or standardized article to be regulated. The regulatory focus may then be on process standards rather than product standards.

"This trend toward an increasing interaction of pharmaceuticals and hardware seems inexorable, as does the expanded reliance on computer software with treatment algorithms."

Hybrid Drug-Devices. Technology is blurring the line drawn by the Federal Food, Drug, and Cosmetic Act between drugs and medical devices in various ways. The software packages that accompany diagnostic equipment may contain treatment algorithms advising on and monitoring the results of drug therapy. Some devices continuously monitor pharmacokinetic or pharmacodynamic parameters and automatically adjust the amount or rate of drug administration with no human intervention (e.g., implantable infusion pumps). Some tools are effective for certain purposes only when used with a drug, such as positron emission scanners and combinations of ultraviolet or laser radiation with photosensitizing drugs. This trend toward an increasing interaction of pharmaceuticals and hardware seems inexorable, as does the expanded reliance on computer software with treatment algorithms.

The interchangeability of either part of a hybrid drug-device combination will be a major issue for regulation in the future. For example, can any laser product that emits energy of certain pulse and wavelength be used with a photosensitizing drug, once it has been established that one laser product with those specifications, when used with the drug, is safe and effective? Good standards for both drugs and devices would facilitate the resolution of this question. Furthermore, it is likely that such standards would accelerate the regulatory approvals of technologies that combine drugs and devices in novel ways by reducing the number of issues to be addressed in the review process.

Continued or Expanded Use of Nontraditional Medicines and Therapies. Homeopathic medicine remains popular in Europe and seems to be gaining more popular acceptance in the United States. The rise of nutriceuticals and cosmeceuticals in Europe and the United States shows that dietary supplements remain steadfast in the consumer's therapeutic armamentarium. The National Institutes of Health is reportedly going to undertake a study of the effectiveness of acupuncture, and "new age" thinking encourages the use of pyramids and crystals.

Although these nontraditional therapies may not be the products of new technology, they will have a significant impact on emerging ideas about health care and, thus, about the regulation of health care technology. As explained earlier, to a large degree this category of product has benefitted from a benign neglect by the FDA, which, in turn, is due to the limited amount of popular support for government intervention into what has been generally perceived as a zone of self-autonomy. These political forces, as well as either real safety concerns (e.g., l-tryptophan) or a fear that patients will pass by effective therapies for the unproved (e.g., laetrile), will undoubtedly influence the future directions of regulation. Were scientific researchers to focus attention on this area, however, and prove either clear patient benefits (perhaps from a placebo response or a holistic medical approach) or clear lack of benefits, the political climate would change. The current statutes can allow regulation that would drive the ineffective from the market; whether they can equally accommodate regulation that accepts a placebo response or other nonpharmacological/nonsurgical reason as a therapeutic benefit to patients is less clear. In the latter situation, the role of a third party in establishing standards for the product and its labeling may be essential to avoid distorting the basic structure of the Federal Food, Drug, and Cosmetic Act.

CONCLUSION

It is argued that:

1. The fundamental social purpose underlying drug and device regulation is not likely to change meaningfully in the next 30 years. The public will still expect that third parties, disinterested in the economic profits to be gained from commercial marketing of drugs and devices, will ensure some level of safety, effectiveness, and quality to prevent harm to and exploitation of patients.
2. The basic regulatory concepts—public standards, premarket approval, process-oriented requirements, and active third-party participation in industry decisions—will be invoked in varying manifestations and combinations to meet emerging problems, real or perceived.
3. Apart from unpredictable health crises, there are certain long-term economic and social forces that will inexorably affect and shape the regulation of drugs and devices during the next 30 years. In addition, technology will provide ever-changing opportunities for and challenges to society in achieving its fundamental objectives and maintaining its values.

If these arguments are valid, what can be predicted about the face of regulation in 2020?

First, the FDA will not have a monopoly on regulatory responsibilities. Other government and private bodies will be vital components.

Second, the public objectives of regulation will expand beyond safety, effectiveness, and quality to include important economic goals, such as ensuring that new therapies are more cost-effective than the ones they are to replace and ensuring that regulatory review processes do not jeopardize the survival of the industries being regulated.

From these two observations, it can be speculated that industry, government, consumers, and taxpayers would welcome the active involvement of private, independent third-party organizations in establishing standards for products and processes. These bodies can move more quickly than can government bureaucracies to adopt and modify rules in light of changing needs and problems. Their standards can have a transnational impact. Finally, standards can facilitate the tasks of compliance and enforcement, thereby making essential and nondelegable government activities more efficient.

DISCUSSION SUMMARY

William Vodra (Partner, Arnold & Porter) stated the basic premise that the law is a tool by which society accomplishes certain ends. Regulation is a legally established tool that society uses essentially to intervene between (1) suppliers of goods and services and (2) consumers of those goods and services to provide some benefit to consumers that they are perceived as being unable to achieve for themselves. In the health care field, there are many types of regulators other than the FDA, such as licensing boards, clinical laboratories, and insurers. Regulation is not necessarily a government function, however. It may be the responsibility of a private organization.

"In the health care field, there are many types of regulators other than the FDA, such as licensing boards, clinical laboratories, and insurers."

John Bergen (Executive Director, National Committee for Clinical Laboratory Standards) reacted to Vodra's paper by commenting that debate on the application of the various regulatory and standards-setting tools may be extensive, but changes are likely to be not revolutionary, but evolutionary. This may tighten the reins on the expansive approaches to health care discussed earlier.

Environmental factors will certainly have an impact on global standardization, according to Bergen. In the United States, the government, industry, and standards-setting organizations are all devoting extensive efforts to harmonization of standards. Harmonized standards are defined as compatible, but not necessarily identical, requirements, and are a vital key to economic globalization. Voluntary international efforts toward standardization are under way, coordinated by the International Standards Organization (ISO) and the International Electrotechnical Commission (IEC). Because of the European drive toward economic unity, European efforts are likely to dominate these standardization activities in both volume and intensity over the next few years.

There are two underlying concepts in the ISO-9000 series of standards, Bergen continued. The most important is the quality system approach; the other is third-party assessment. The first is founded on the assumption that, if the production and management system is right, then the product or service that it produces will also be right. The system builds quality in, rather than screening error out. The second concept operates under the rationale that it is better to have a third party determine the appropriateness of a system than to have individual purchasers carry out their own supplier assessments independently.

Bergen concluded by saying that, in the United States, the underlying regulatory concepts are unlikely to change significantly. These concepts are not consistent with the European approach, however. The U.S. standards-setting organizations need to expand their interregional and international focus, without eroding their basic efforts, in order to ensure a leadership position. The challenge to these organizations is to become a positive force in bridging the U.S. basic regulatory and standards-setting concepts with the prevailing and evolving international efforts that focus on quality systems.

J. Richard Crout (Vice President, Medical and Scientific Affairs, Boehringer Mannheim Pharmaceutical) agreed with Vodra that no one in the industry seems to want a revolution in regulation. Although the general regulatory structure will not change, it is likely to evolve to take into account new technologies, gene therapies, and cellular therapies, for example. He described three factors that will affect regulation. First, product liability is a significant deterrent to product development in the United States today. Tort reform is essential. Crout predicted that, some time in the next 25 years, society will find a legislative solution to the problem of product liability so that the system will no longer revolve around a victim's compensation. Second, private sector regulation will increase so that the role of formulary committees, prudent buyers, and others will become more important. In this case, the role of the FDA will decline. Nongovernmental organizations will have to plan for this opportunity and responsibility. Third, the style of regulation is likely to change so that consensus building becomes the fundamental mechanism for decision making.

"Private sector regulation will increase so that the role of formulary committees, prudent buyers, and others will become more important."

According to Louis Lasagna (Dean, Sackler School of Graduate Biomedical Science, Tufts University), the approval of drugs is not now based on a formal decision analysis. This poses problems when patient advocates, sponsors, or other groups disagree with a decision of the FDA. Approval is currently based on standards of average performance, massified data, the "herd response" (i.e., appropriate for the "average" person), rather than an individual response. This approach leaves unanswered a physician's question about how to treat a particular patient. It is necessary, Lasagna suggested, to do more "data dredging," that is, searching for determinants of the success or failure of a drug based on the differing characteristics of the patients. Lasagna made several other points:

- Official approval often lags behind drug knowledge. At present there is no agreed upon, up-to-date, unassailable authority. Although not easy, it is important to establish such an authority. Multiple authorities are likely to complicate the issues.
- The education of the public may be less important than the education of public health officials and politicians. Vaccines, for example, protect both the individual and the herd, partly because people are told what to do.
- User fees for competent, talented individuals who can conduct an outside review may expedite the drug approval process.
- Federal legislation may allow a state-of-the-art defense and deny punitive damages for drug injury. The United States

appears to be moving in that direction state by state, but a uniform federal law could be helpful.

- There is no reason to assume that finding the genetic locus of a disease is translatable into a patient benefit. Eventually this may happen, but it is impossible to predict.

Lasagna concluded by asking what the ethical implications are for society when the cheapest available treatment is not the best available treatment.

Emmanuel Somers (Director General, Drugs Directorate, Health and Welfare Canada) identified four issues that will have to be examined if the future is not to be just like the present. First, global harmonization is proceeding because the Japanese and the European Community want it. In order to be a full partner, the United States must change its perspective of industry and become more responsive to industry's analyses. Ironically, the United States is the most capitalistic of the advanced countries, but the cooperation between its drug regulators and industry is among the lowest of the major countries. With or without the United States as a full partner, however, this is harmonization by the rich. Second, patients are pushing for faster evaluation of drugs. Third, risk categorization is likely to be important in the future if regulation is to be more rational; not all drugs and medical devices are equally dangerous. It is essential to examine the social implications of risk. Finally, the cost of drugs should be tied to their effectiveness.

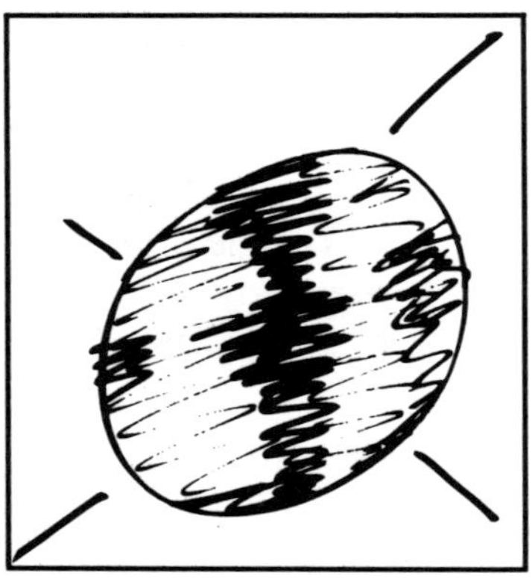

"In a global system of regulation, not all countries have the therapeutic, economic, and political infrastructure to make maximum use of pharmaceuticals. . ."

In discussing an anticipated global system of regulation, Rosalyn King (Director, International Health Institute, Charles R. Drew University of Medicine and Science) remarked that, while this would have a positive effect on the pharmaceuticals themselves, there are several limiting factors. Not all countries have the therapeutic, economic, administrative, and political infrastructure to make maximum use of those pharmaceuticals that have been standardized; some of the undeveloped countries, for example, must still cope with the lack of water and other resources essential to sound hygiene practices. In addition, when the developed countries export assistance, they export their own patterns and practices, which may not fit into those of the undeveloped countries. In response, Leighton noted that administrative integration and standardization are not necessarily linked and that it is certainly possible for each country to maintain its own regulatory authority while scientific standards are uniform.

Vodra commented that several Third World countries are already willing to accept products from other countries if those products have the approval of two or three of the major First World regulatory agencies. Problems arise in the United States, however, in regard to the importation of drugs that have been standardized under different systems. An organization such as the ISO, established in part to resolve the problems that have arisen because of fragmented European production standards, may be the answer, but, as Thomas Layloff (Director, Division of Drug Analysis, FDA) noted, there is no way to enforce standards across national boundaries.

The role of outside organizations in setting standards may expand, according to Judy Boehlert (Assistant Vice President and Director, Hoffmann-La Roche). At the present time, each manufacturer of pharmaceuticals must go out and find qualified suppliers of the raw materials. It would seem to make sense to have an international organization that would qualify suppliers and reduce the duplicated efforts of the individual manufacturers and, thus, the cost. It would also make sense for an outside organization to establish international standards for drugs and dosage forms.

Standards setting and regulation will need to reflect the merger of formerly separate items. Many therapies involve drugs, devices, and technologies that are not clearly separate. A treatment such as positron emission tomography (PET), for example, may involve more than one regulatory department. The scanners are regulated as devices, while the radiopharmaceuticals used are regulated as drugs. They are one system, however, and cannot be used separately. It makes no sense, according to one participant, to consider such a system as a product; Vodra proposed that it should be treated as a therapeutic modality. Somers added that it is now impossible to continue the facade that all these products can be controlled with our limited resources. The European model, which has a much closer alliance with industry, may be at least part of the answer to this problem.

The public is not impotent, Lasagna commented. The AIDS story has demonstrated the effectiveness of patient advocacy. The public can demand explanations of delays in drug approval and participate in useful debates about the appropriate timing of a drug's release for clinical use. Although there are hazards associated with public involvement in judgment calls, the public can have an impact on the FDA.

The United States has an enormous risk aversion. It is really not possible, however, to find *all* the side effects. Even so, any unfortunate effects that occur after a drug has been approved seem to lead to punitive measures. Changes may allow the system to act more efficiently on the basis of less information. Crout added that people want more input into regulatory decisions, more information about each drug, data on cost-effectiveness, and quality of life; this cannot be accomplished quickly. Furthermore, this is not the purview of drug regulation, but of drug development and societal desires. The real issue is, "What can be given up in order to achieve rapid drug approvals?"

The FDA is becoming even more conservative and even more cautious, another participant noted. Marcus observed that requirements for disease-specific data for simple diagnostic agents, such as X-ray contrast media, that have nearly a zero probability of adverse effect are also driving up the cost of drug development. It may not be possible to make the process faster; it may be necessary to limit the knowledge requirements. Lasagna commented that the FDA should not be unchallengeable in the information requirements that it establishes; challenge is necessary to open up the process. Somers added that the British model has fewer than one-tenth the reviewers and drugs are approved much more quickly with not much more hazard to the public.

Vodra stated that the whole system would change radically if the health care delivery and financing system would eliminate issues such as fault. It would then be possible to eliminate the fault-finding process that generates the political oversight that causes the FDA to search for more data. More fundamentally, a reversion to pre-World War II attitudes about death and dying when death is perceived as part of the natural process will lead to very basic changes in our views of risk and drug regulation.

Trachtenberg expressed some concern that underdeveloped countries are being considered (1) as a source of new materials and (2) as a place to conduct clinical trials that may be considered unethical in the developed world. The issue of giving the people in these countries access to the drugs that they are being used to develop requires more consideration. In the area of information and standards, simple translations of materials may be helpful, according to Marcus. There must be means to provide information to the poor and the uneducated in the Third World countries and in the United States. Nongovernmental organizations such as the USP may have a role to play in providing this information.

"Many standards are actually educational tools. In these terms, even future individualized treatments will require standards to help providers use these treatments appropriately and effectively."

In response to a question from one participant, Bezold defined standards as identity, strength, purity, packaging, and labeling for pharmaceuticals as they are now known. Process standards are now challenging these product-specific standards. Part of the future standards question is, What is needed to define a therapeutic modality so that it is uniform and effective in each use? In addition, it is necessary to answer the question, What are the information systems necessary to ensure the wise use of health care technology in the future? The scope of information is likely to be broader than that of standards.

One participant noted that American Society for Testing Materials (ASTM), the largest of the more than 300 standards-setting organizations in the United States, has four categories: (1) standard procedures, (2) standard specifications, (3) standard definitions, and (4) standard guides. Many standards are actually educational tools. In these terms, even future individualized treatments will require standards to help providers use these treatments appropriately and effectively. Thus, in certain areas, standards and information are merging. Another participant commented that the form of standards is likely to be different in the future. Information published by organizations such as the USP is likely to become standards. It may be necessary, therefore, to have standards to ensure the quality of information systems as well.

Yarbro noted that cost constraints seem likely to permeate all areas of health care and that the rapid transmission of information about genuine improvements in pharmaceuticals will be unprecedented. Yet, regulation seems unlikely to improve and may grow worse.

Joseph Valentino (Associate Executive Director, USP) commented that standards and information are not clearly distinct. Information should be examined in terms of who is using it—health care providers, health educators, clinical pharmacists, or patients. Consumers may or may not need scientific information, but they should have a mechanism to determine that providers, for example, meet certain requirements (e.g., certification or practice outcomes). Sometimes the focus of discussion seems to be on the delivery of information rather than its use in the decision-making process.

6

Ideal Designs for Standards and Information in 2020: Strategic Implications

by Clement Bezold, Ph.D., and Gail Martin

Having explored the wide range of factors that may affect standards and information, USP 2020 participants were asked to design ideal systems for standards and information for health care technology in 2020. They were asked to consider what may occur and to identify the best systems. This request is difficult for most people to respond to because it is an unfamiliar task. As one member of the group put it, "You want me to create the system as if I were king!" Yet designing ideal systems and turning those into visions that drive your strategies is a very important process.

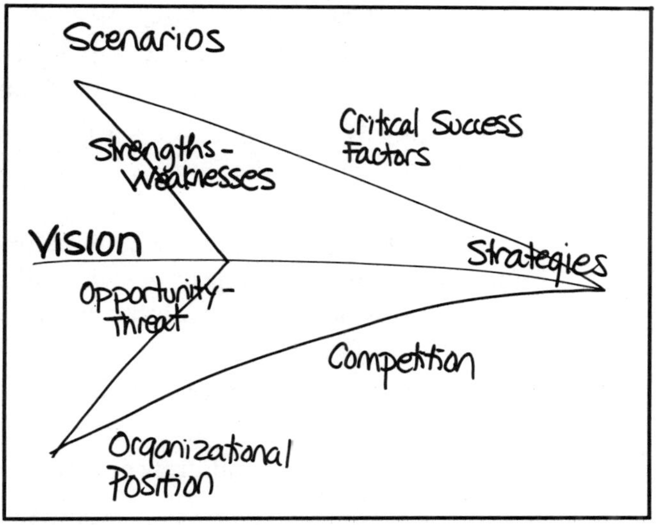

Small groups integrated the scenarios, papers, and discussions and generated their visions of "ideal" standards and/or information system designs.

The Conference participants divided into four

small groups, with two focusing on ideal systems for standards, one on an information system, and one on both. In addition to developing the framework of their ideal system, the small groups were asked to identify (1) the biggest changes in their system, (2) the legacy of which they would be most proud, and (3) their most significant breakthroughs.

Group A Ideal Design: Standards

In its vision of the future, Group A saw a "system of establishing and disseminating officially recognized standards of quality and authoritative information for the use of articles of health care technology by practitioners, patients, and consumers." They based the vision on the following design principles:

- a voluntary and nongovernmental system
- collaboration of industry, academia, professional disciplines, and government agencies
- adaptability to change
- flexibility to meet the needs of the health care system, such as an urgent need for treatment of specific diseases (e.g., AIDS)
- evolution from a national system to a regional, i.e., hemispheric system, and, ultimately, to a global system
- development of confidence, trust, and integrity through actions
- inclusion of standards for articles and processes in the production of all pharmaceuticals, whether homeopathic, allopathic, nutriceutical, or botanical; biologics; diagnostic and medical devices; or any other substance or technology (but not cosmetics)
- recognition of both conventional and nontraditional forms of health care
- recognition of ethnic differences with multilingual components
- safeguards from conflict of interest
- enforcement of standards by government agency or agencies

To comply with these principles, Group A noted that the following key actions would be necessary:

- enhancement of collegial relationships among all stakeholders
- legislation
- restructuring of government agencies
- demonstration of quality performance to engender public trust
- definition of the scope of the system and development of the necessary strategic plan
- increased communication with all other pharmacopeias globally

The group described the biggest changes from the present as its vision's greater collaboration between private and government agencies, including international entities; empowerment of stakeholders for self-determination; and increased quality standards for homeopathic, nutriceutical, and botanical products. Group A considered public trust the most important legacy of its system. Its members also believed that their system encouraged a movement from confrontation to collaboration and allowed innovation while maintaining public health and welfare. As a comprehensive system for health care technology standards, it encompassed research and education, both public and professional.

The most significant breakthroughs, the group believed, would be enabling legislation for the system, an increase in public trust, a streamlined process of standards setting as a result of bringing standards under one body, and increased globalization.

One participant commented that, because the standards-setting organizations in this model are nongovernmental, it may be easier for them to form a global network.

Group A considered legislation necessary to expand current standards mandates and authorize standards setting for new developments in technology. In addition, enabling legislation may be needed to clarify the lines between standards setting by a voluntary, nongovernmental organization and enforcement by the government and to establish a system of checks and balances.

Group B Ideal Design: Information Systems

One group designed an information system incorporating non-governmental control, an accountability and liability balance scheme to deal with confidentiality issues, and a marketing and distribution strategy for health data and databases (DB).

The design principles outlined by Group B for a health information system in 2020 included:

- empowerment of individuals to deal more effectively with health issues
- privacy and confidentiality of personal health information
- security/error checking
- universality of access
- diversity of information on a particular health issue, which may require multiple databases and may permit some chaos in the information
- a continuous validation process with an indication of the information's level of validity
- associative search capability
- tiers of information so that individuals obtain the level of information appropriate to their understanding (e.g., more detailed level of information for a physician)

- interactive databases that allow self-learning
- virtual reality that demonstrates the health consequences of particular behaviors and therapies
- integration into an optimal health care system
- a comprehensive database that includes international data and allows global access and input
- self-checking communications protocols
- cost-effectiveness
- ability to track all health factors

"The most significant breakthroughs would be the enhancement of cognitive capability for the public, policy makers, and health care providers, and the creation of a nongovernmental organization to manage the health information system in a way that would engender public trust."

One of the key actions that Group B advocated to bring its vision to fruition was the creation of a designated institution to guarantee that the envisioned database is not politically biased. Because of concern that government management of the database would interfere with empowerment, the group believed that a nongovernmental institution should operate the entire information system. Enabling legislation might be necessary, according to its members, not to create the institution, but to remove barriers to its formation. For example, it might be necessary to enact legislation to permit the inclusion of private information in the system.

Members of the group were also concerned about liability exposure as a result of individual interaction with the system that may lead to an unfortunate occurrence. A scheme to balance accountability and liability would be phased in between now and 2020. A financing strategy, preferably nongovernmental, and a marketing/distribution strategy were also part of the vision. In addition to the empowerment of individuals, Group B's model might both provide education and assist policy makers and decision makers; these latter functions were secondary, however.

The biggest changes from the present were in the creation of a credible, independent, and effective health information system that would lead to individual empowerment and engagement. The most significant breakthroughs were the enhancement of cognitive capability for the public, policy makers, and health care providers, and the creation of a nongovernmental organization to manage the health information system in a way that would engender public trust. The measure of success would be in the degree of improvement of the quality of life.

Group C Ideal Design: Information System and Standards

After some debate about the need for two models, one for standards and one for information, Group C decided that standards and information could be included in one model. In the design principles for its vision of an optimum health information system in 2020, Group C included the following:

- patient-driven system
- comprehensive, continuous evaluation
- outcomes-based design
- no barriers to access (i.e., user-friendly)
- collaborative, multidisciplinary decision-making process
- merger and constant evolution of standards and information
- consideration of international factors

Patient needs and values, patient outcomes, patient knowledge and decision making, and patient economics were the boundaries of Group C's design. No processes occurred outside these boundaries.

Innovation, driven by patient needs, values, and economics, passed to an eclectic collection of standards-setting organizations, clinical societies, patient representatives, payers, economists, regulators, suppliers, researchers, and others, who made decisions in a collaborative process.

This group presented standards, although the word *standards* in this design was expanded to include not only the declarative statements that currently make up standards, but also the information that leads to standards and, perhaps, all the information that is necessary to implement and evaluate those standards. At this point in the vision, "standards" were broken into two components: (1) information used to promote the use and recognition of the standard by patients and (2) the actual standard used by effectors, such as providers. The process then circulated back through patient outcomes.

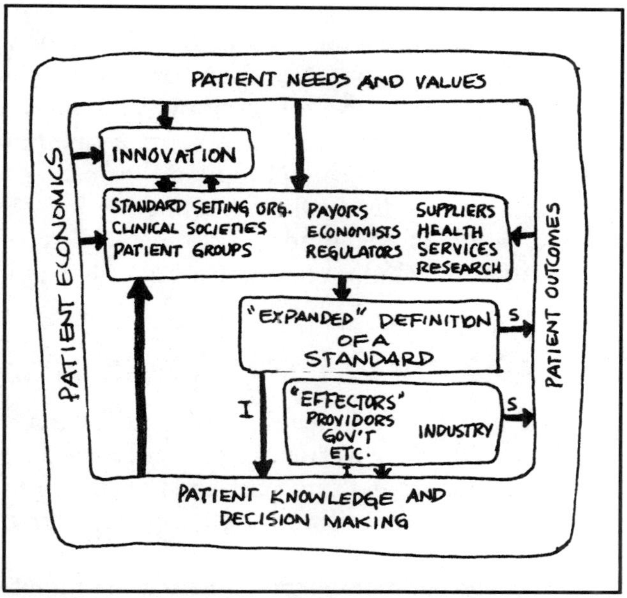

Expanded patient emphasis, new therapies, a collaborative infrastructure, and continuous monitoring framed one group's design for a combined standards and information system for the future.

The key actions that Group C considered necessary to achieve this vision included:

- increased involvement of the patient through education and value formation
- improved record keeping and analysis
- expanded monitoring and reporting
- functional measurement (i.e., in terms of the quality of life)
- universal availability of information
- broadened representation
- expanded scope

- harmonization efforts/international cultural adaptation
- new product development that leads to greater availability

Group C described the biggest changes as a new patient emphasis and orientation; new therapies, many of which will be molecular; a collaborative infrastructure; and continuous monitoring. The most significant breakthroughs were the outcomes-based orientation of the information system, with appropriate technological support, and the emphasis on individualized treatment. Members of Group C were most proud of the fluidity and adaptability of their design and its potential contribution to improved global health.

Group D Ideal Design: Standards

In view of the technical and scientific expertise and functions that exist outside the government, Group D saw an evolution to a coalition of standards-setting organizations to respond to various agencies and regulators. Among other design principles, the group included:

- recognition of government accountability for policy decisions
- formal recognition that technical and scientific functions can be delegated to nongovernment bodies
- inclusion of standards for all health care products and services; although there was a lack of consensus on "all," the group agreed that software, devices, drugs, and biologics should go through this system
- greater reliance on horizontal, or process-setting, standards
- the degree of risk associated with health care products as the basis of standards setting for those products
- international harmonization

Group D saw an evolution to a "stop-cock" system that contained current information about standards for a variety of health care components, ranging from product manufacturing and design through study-specific protocols, research and development, data presentation and analysis, risk assessment, labeling, outcomes, and reimbursement criteria to postmarket surveillance. The interactor with this health information system was not the patient, but the person with the new idea. With the availability of very current criteria, technical experts in

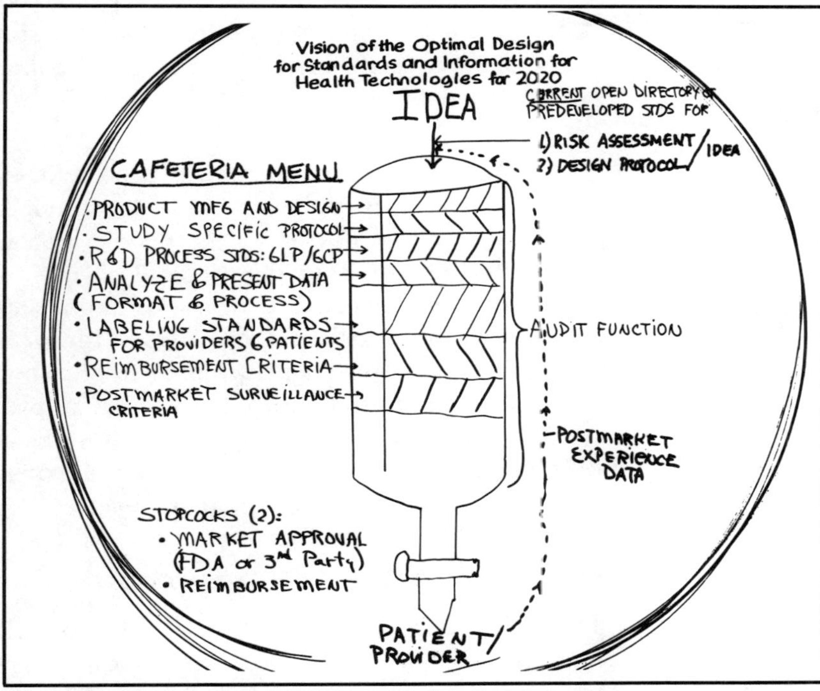

This "Stop Cock" model of standards setting and regulation would be driven by degree of risk and would separate technical/scientific and political/regulatory functions.

one organization could advise an innovator on the appropriate areas to select from the information/regulation flow. This would facilitate the design of protocols and the assessment of risk.

Group D agreed that getting to market was synonymous with getting payer approval. Group members also agreed that a great deal of data would cycle into the system. A viable additional role for the non-governmental standards-setting organization might be an audit function. Such an audit function could be a source of income for the organization.

The group described the biggest changes in this design as the greatly expanded role of nongovernmental experts, the coalition of non-governmental standards-setting groups, the expansion to other health care products, and the audit function. The significant breakthrough was in separating technical and scientific functions from political and regulatory functions. The legacy of Group D's design was in tailoring regulatory standards to relative risk and in promoting international harmonization.

"The legacy of Group D's design was in tailoring regulatory standards to relative risk and in promoting international harmonization."

One member commented that current, up-to-date, state-of-the-art thoughts cannot be obtained by having all the people who set the rules reside on the federal payroll. In this vision, technical decisions about standards become the responsibility of those outside the government, while decisions about whether a product reaches the marketplace remain the responsibility of politically accountable authorities. The pool of experts then becomes larger and more diverse.

Development of Whole Group Vision

The discussions and the ideal designs of the small groups served as the basis for the Conference participants as a whole to explore the aspects that would define the whole group's shared vision for standards and

Vision: An accessible, universal system that is patient-driven and empowers the public.

information. When asked to name the components that they found most compelling in the small group visions, the Conference participants noted the desirability of having an accessible, universal system that is patient-driven and empowers the public. They also considered the following components desirable:

- empowerment of *all* participants
- helpfulness and responsiveness to all stakeholders
- comprehensive, accessible, and outcome-driven standards that respect individualized treatment and care, and improve public health
- globalization of the system that provides standards and information that increases public health and welfare
- cooperation and coalition of international groups
- risk assessment as a guiding principle for the complexity of standards and regulation of health care product development
- separation of scientific and technical expertise from government regulation
- open, interactive process with continuous revision
- confidentiality capability

There was a division among the participants at this point. Some felt that the focus should be on standards, not on information. This led to an extended debate about the need for a confidentiality capability in the health information system of the future. Several participants stated that the system should contain only public information, which would make a confidentiality capability unnecessary. Others noted that private information can be "sanitized" for the public; for example, the system might contain the number of people who have AIDS, but no identifying information on these individuals. Those who believed that the optimum system is to be used by an individual who should have access to all information and who should be able to share his or her personal information through the system with a health care provider supported a built-in confidentiality capability. Others believed that the system should not deal with the physician-patient link and, therefore, needs no such capability.

Thus, in developing standards for health technologies, there were two minds. One was that a vision can be developed only up to a defined point, involving only standards; the other group felt that standards and information systems cannot ultimately be separated and, therefore, it is necessary to have a vision for the whole piece, including the patient's use. One participant emphasized that the risk of allowing the information system to substitute for human beings who provide health care makes it essential for the system to be compatible with the health care system. Another participant suggested that there should be a distinction between information for well people and information for sick people, although the information system may serve as the first line of care for sick people (i.e., when to consult a health care provider).

Conference participants noted the desirability of having an accessible, universal, system that is patient-driven and empowers the public.

In view of the similarities between the visions of Groups B and C, an effort was made to combine the two models in a way that would resolve the disagreement. The center of the resulting model, as described by McDonald, was an intelligent system that includes humans and machines working together on a database derived from all over the world; the government, health care provider, patient, and medical expert systems were connected to the database and linked to each other around it. This design allowed patients to have direct access to the system for information, although the patient's link to the medical expert system might be around the database, not necessarily through it.

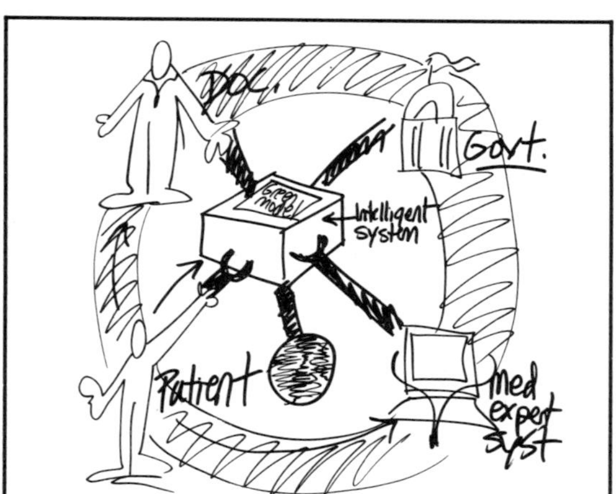

Combining the visions of two groups produced an outline of an integrated health information and standards system for health care technology.

The participants were almost evenly divided in their support of this vision. Some thought that the patient should be the center and that the standards and information systems should revolve around the person. Others thought that the system should be more limited. As one participant explained the disagreement, "one group is focusing on the box in the center, and the other group is focusing on the rest of it." It was suggested that the lesson of this disagreement is that the context for standards in 2020 is likely to be broader than our view in the early 1990s.

In considering the optimum system for standards per se, the discussion returned to the vision of Group A. One member described the group's vision of a 2020 system as regional on the way to global. National barriers would begin to erode, and the collaboration of the various stakeholders would increase. This vision depended on enhanced collegial relationships. The basis would be an improved interaction between government actions and private sector responsibility and credibility. Standards-setting, monitoring, and auditing responsibilities would become the responsibilities of a private organization. The system would be very sensitive to innovation, and new technologies would perhaps become a more active focus of government activities. When these new technologies were accepted, they would move to the private sector. The group considered it possible, however, that new health care products approval processes could move out of the realm of government.

Vodra suggested that the ready availability of information on all the aspects of bringing new technologies to market, as visualized by Group D (see the "stop-cock" model on page 195), might minimize the time that the manufacturers of new technologies need to reach the market. The person who used the standards in this system would be the innovator. The current definition of standards, which focuses primarily on product specifications, would be expanded to include process specifications. All standards-setting and regulatory bodies would be a part of this system. Such a coalition would allow "one-stop shopping" for a manufacturer, providing all the necessary information in one place and, thus, increasing competitiveness.

The cafeteria menu of tests, standards, and regulations for each product would be based on primary risk assessment. A broader range of both products and processes in health care would be involved, according to one participant. Although the same standards would not apply to everything, the approach to standardization would have some commonalities. For example, evaluations of the identity and purity of drugs would apply to all drugs, whether allopathic, homeopathic, prescription, cosmeceutical, or nutriceutical. Standards for software should also be part of the system.

"The cafeteria menu of tests, standards, and regulations for each product would be based on primary risk assessment."

Northup commented that the major differences in the various models lie in the time line.

The dilemma among the participants lay in a difference of opinion regarding how broad the boundaries of the health information system of the future should be. Several organizations have found it necessary to provide information as well as standards. Thus, some participants began with the current concept of standards, while others removed the boundaries in order to provide information that empowers patients.

One participant expressed some concern that the vision shows a system designed primarily for "yuppies" with computers, that only 10% to 15% of the lay population of the United States will be able to use it, and that social justice was not addressed in any of the models. Another participant responded that the focus of the Conference was on "the best that could be." He noted that there is a difference between accessibility and distribution.

Ullman noted that it is necessary to be open to new types of therapies. Medical practice in 2020 is likely to be drastically different from medical practice today. A commitment to innovation is essential. New categories of regulation may be helpful. One of the problems in regulation is the lack of an area between foods and drugs; there is no middle ground for "natural medicines," which are substances that have therapeutic value and are more than foods or supplements. This was a constraint on the exercises that took place during the Conference, according to Ullman.

In order to promote equity, McDonald suggested involvement in the production of new software that would allow communities to determine their own outcomes data and their own utilization of drugs and devices. Then it would be possible to compare communities.

In relating the scenarios that were presented at the opening of the Conference to the visions, Bezold commented that the broader of the small group ideal designs appeared closer to the preferred scenarios of global business and a new social contract. The more narrow visions for standards, while still a stretch from the present, are more consistent with the scenarios that the Conference participants considered more likely to occur, that is, hard times and high technology.

"Those with broader vision perceived information needs as individual-oriented, patient-driven, and outcome-driven; in this vision there is a greater number of stakeholders. Those who focused on standards foresaw a more limited universe of stakeholders and a more limited horizon of what is necessary to make the system work well."

Halperin commented that the basic difference in the visions was in the groups' views of standards and information. Those with the broader vision perceived information needs as individual-oriented, patient-driven, and outcome-driven; in this vision, there is a greater number of stakeholders. Those who focused on standards foresaw a more limited universe of stakeholders and a more limited horizon of what is necessary to make the system work well. McDonald added that standards may be broadened, however, to relate to the populations that use them.

In reacting to the Conference, Gina Kolata (Science Writer, *New York Times*) commented on the enormous hunger of individuals for more information. She was particularly enthusiastic about the information systems in which patients have access. She observed that there is a natural tension between the federal government and nongovernmental organizations and the industry that is consistent with the scenarios and that suggest that visions of the role of groups outside the government be enlarged in the drug evaluation and approval process.

In his closing remarks, Bezold described a compelling vision as one that establishes a creative tension between what exists now and what is desirable. Something that is easy is not a stretch. The job of a leader is to manage that creative tension. The standards and information community will need to decide on its vision and to determine how best to provide leadership.

In closing the Conference, Halperin noted the uncertainty in the future of standards and information, and his own hope that the community's vision will not "stay within the lines."

Appendix I

About the United States Pharmacopeial Convention, Inc., Institute for Alternative Futures, Authors and Editors

The United States Pharmacopeial Convention, Inc. (USP), established in 1820, is an independent, not-for-profit organization comprising members from the health care professions and sciences representing academia, industry, and government. USP promotes the public health by establishing and disseminating officially recognized standards of quality and authoritative information for the use of medicines and related articles by health care professionals, patients, and consumers. The standards are published in the *United States Pharmacopeia* and the *National Formulary (USP-NF)* and drug-use information is provided in the *USP DI.*

The Institute for Alternative Futures (IAF) is a nonprofit think tank in Alexandria, Virginia that assists communities and organizations to more wisely choose and create the futures they prefer. Founded by Alvin Toffler, Clement Bezold, and James Dator, IAF works with governments at all levels (from municipal governments to the World Health Organization) and throughout the U.S. and Europe. IAF has done extensive research on the future of health care, pharmaceuticals, information and communication, and government. IAF develops forecasts of key trends and scenarios and works with individuals and organizations to develop their visions of the ideal futures they want to create. IAF's for profit subsidiary, Alternative Futures Associates, provides similar services to large corporations in the U.S. and Europe.

Clement Bezold, Ph.D., Executive Director of the Institute for Alternative Futures and President of Alternative Futures Associates, is a political scientist and futurist who has worked and written extensively on the future of government, health care, work and the legal system. He is a consultant to governors and state legislatures, hospital and pharmaceutical companies, and professional associations. His books include **Anticipatory Democracy, Pharmaceuticals in the Year 2000, Pharmacy in the 21st Century** (co-edited with Jerome Halperin, Howard L. Binkley, and Richard R. Ashbaugh), and **The Future of Work and Health** (co-authored with Rick Carlson and Jonathan Peck), which won **American Health** magazine's book award. Dr. Bezold is the government editor of **The Futurist**, and has also published numerous articles on future trends for magazines such as **Business and Health**, and **Modern Health Care**.

Russell C. Coile, Jr., M.B.A., a futurist specializing in the health industry, is the President of the Health Forecasting Group, which provides market forecasts and strategic advice to a wide range of U.S. health care companies. He is a frequent speaker and author on aspects of health and the future. Prior to forming his own consulting firm, Mr. Coile established the first corporate futures program in the Health industry for the Lutheran Hospital Society of Southern California, where he was the Director of the Center for Health Management Research. Mr. Coile is the author of both **The New Hospital: Future Strategies for a Changing Industry**, and **The New Medicine: Reshaping Medical Practice and Healthcare Management**, co-author of **Introduction to Health Planning**, and editor of the **Hospital Strategy Report** by Aspen Publishers. He is also a member of the editorial advisory boards of **Modern Healthcare, Managed Care Outlook**, and **Healthcare Competition Week**. Mr. Coile's columns, "Future Track" and "The Leading Edge," appear regularly in **Healthcare Forum Journal**.

Stuart N. Davidson is the Executive Director of the Center For Technology Assessment, a part of the St. Joseph Health System of Orange, California, a not-for-profit health care corporation with hospitals and other health care installation laboratories in California and Texas. The Center was founded in 1983 to stimulate continuing studies of scientific research in the delivery of health care. For twenty-five years, prior to his retirement in December 1982, Mr. Davidson was with Beckman Instruments, ultimately serving as Corporate Director of Government Affairs. From 1976–1982, he served as a Trustee of the St. Jude Hospital and Rehabilitation Center. During 1982, Mr. Davidson served on the Grace Commission, which submitted to President Reagan, in 1982, a report making 2000 recommendations concerning better management practices necessary to bring government spending under control. His particular responsibility was to review and report to the President the state of our nation's science research and to make recommendations for future action. He is author of a regular newsletter on health technology trends, **St. Joseph Health System Technology Assessment Newsletter**, and of a forthcoming book, **System 2020 AD.**

Jacqueline L. Eng joined the U.S. Pharmacopeial Convention, Inc. in 1992 as Assistant Executive Director for Professional and Public Affairs. In this position she is responsible for directing USP's external affairs with national professional and trade associations, state pharmaceutical and medical associations, educational institutions, the media, and the public. She joined USP following seven years as Director of Public Affairs for the American Association of Colleges of Pharmacy and six years as Assistant Director for Public Affairs at the Nonprescription Drug Manufacturers Association. Ms. Eng also served as an Information Officer for the Food and Drug Administration. In addition to her press officer responsibilities at FDA, she developed agency education programs for both consumers and health care professionals and also served as Director of the Agency's Freedom of Information Office. Ms. Eng has been involved in the development of regulatory and legislative policy and has worked extensively with the media and governmental, professional, higher education, and health care communities.

Jerome A. Halperin was appointed Executive Director of the United States Pharmacopeial Convention, Inc. in March 1990. In this position he also serves as Chairman of the General Committee of Revision, Secretary of the Board of Trustees, and Secretary of the USP Convention. He joined USP following six years in the pharmaceutical industry as Vice President-Technology for CIBA Consumer Pharmaceuticals, a division of CIBA-GEIGY, Inc. As a commissioned officer in the U.S. Public Health Service, he served as a pharmacist in the Indian Health Service and Marine hospitals and as a radiological health specialist. In 1974 he joined the headquarters staff of the Food and Drug Administration as Deputy Associate Director for New Drug Evaluation (Scientific) of the Bureau of Drugs, attaining the position of Director of the Office of Drugs of the National Center for Drugs and Biologics prior to leaving the Agency in 1983. Mr. Halperin earned his B.S. in pharmacy from Rutgers, The State University of New Jersey; M.P.H. from The Johns Hopkins School of Hygiene and Public Health; and S.M. in Management at the Massachusetts Institute of Technology.

Gail W. Martin, a graduate of Brown University, has 20 years of experience in all forms of writing, editing, and proofreading. Although her range of experience includes publications in the areas of law and education, she specializes in publications in the health care field. Her clients have included physicians and health care organizations from all over the United States.

Michael McDonald, M.P.H., is President of Windom Health Enterprises, and Health and Human Ecology Director of the Environmental Science and Policy Institute (ESPI). Internationally recognized for his pioneering work in health promotion communications technologies, Mr. McDonald has been designing and implementing health risk assessment tools since 1978. He has been involved in some of the seminal work done in personal health information systems and PICSELs (Public Interest Communication Systems and Electronic Libraries). In addition to his work with Windom Health Enterprises and ESPI, Mr. McDonald serves as the 1991/92 Chair of Communications and Computer Applications in Public Health (CCAPH) and is a consultant and service provider to numerous government agencies, corporations, hospitals, and insurance companies in the areas of health communications and the design of health promotion-oriented health systems.

William W. Vodra, J.D. is a Partner in the Washington, D.C. law firm of Arnold & Porter. He is the former Associate Chief Counsel for Drugs with the Food and Drug Administration. While at the FDA, Mr. Vodra was recognized for playing a major role in the development of the Drug Regulatory Reform Act of 1978, as well as his contributions to a variety of programs, such as the good laboratory practice and bioresearch monitoring regulations, generic drug review, and drug quality assurance. Mr. Vodra served as Vice Chairman of the Commission on the Federal Drug Approval Process, established by Congressmen James Scheuer and Albert Gore, to recommend improvements in the FDA's review of new drugs.

Appendix II

Participant List

USP 2020: The Strategic Context of Drug Standards and Drug Information September 9–11, 1992

Banks, Jamie, Senior Associate, Charles River Associates Inc.
Barker, Kenneth N., Ph.D., Professor and Head, Auburn University School of Pharmacy, Department of Pharmacy Care Systems
Bennett, Donald R., M.D., Ph.D., Director, Division of Drugs and Toxicology, American Medical Association
Bergen, John V., Ph.D., Executive Director, National Committee for Clinical Laboratory Standards
Bezold, Clement, Ph.D., Executive Director, Institute for Alternative Futures
Boehlert, Judy, Ph.D., Assistant Vice President, Director, Pharmaceutical Quality Control and Assurance, Hoffmann-La Roche, Inc.
Boylan, James C., Ph.D., Director, Pharmaceutical Research and Development, Abbott Laboratories Hospital Products Division
Bransome, Edwin D., Jr., M.D., Professor of Medicine, Section of Metabolic and Endocrine Disease, Medical College of Georgia
Church, Richard M., Pharm.D., Chief, Pharmacy Program, Indian Health Service
Cohen, Jordan L., Ph.D., Dean, College of Pharmacy, University of Kentucky
Coile, Russell C., Jr., M.B.A., President, Health Forecasting Group
Crout, J. Richard, M.D., Vice President, Medical and Scientific Affairs, Boehringer Mannheim Pharmaceuticals Corporation
Davidson, Stuart N., Director, Center for Technology Assessment, St. Joseph Health System
Doluisio, James T., Ph.D., Dean & Hoechst-Roussel Professor, College of Pharmacy, University of Texas at Austin
Eng, Jacqueline L., Assistant Executive Director for Professional and Public Affairs, U.S. Pharmacopeial Convention, Inc.

Fahy, Gregory M., Ph.D., Biomedical R&D, American Red Cross
Fay, John T., Jr., Ph.D., Corporate Editor, *Wholesale Drugs Magazine*
Feffer, David, Chairman, Employee Managed Care Corporation
Finkelstein, Stanley, M.D., Executive Director, Program on Pharmaceuticals, Massachusetts Institute of Technology
Fitzgerald, Edward A., Ph.D., Director, Division of Product Quality Control, Center for Biologics, Food and Drug Administration
Florey, Klaus G., Ph.D., Consultant, Princeton, New Jersey
Gourley, Dick R., Pharm.D., Professor and Dean, College of Pharmacy, University of Tennessee
Grady, L. Timothy, Ph.D., Director, Drug Standards Division, U.S. Pharmacopeial Convention, Inc.
Guthrie, Robert M., M.D., Associate Professor, College of Medicine, The Ohio State University
Halperin, Jerome A., Executive Director, U.S. Pharmacopeial Convention, Inc.
Hanna, Samir A., Ph.D., Vice President Worldwide Quality Control, Bristol-Myers Squibb Company
Hayes, Arthur Hull, Jr., M.D., President, MediScience Associates
Hoffman, James, M.D., Vice President, Medical Services, DuPont Merck Pharmaceutical Company
Hughes, David W., Ph.D., Special Projects Officer, Health and Welfare, Canada Health Protection Branch
Hulse, James W., Vice President, Quality and Regulatory Affairs, Becton Dickinson and Company
Johnson, Keith W., Director, Drug Information Division, U.S. Pharmacopeial Convention, Inc.
Kahn, Michael G., M.D., Ph.D., Assistant Professor of Medicine, School of Medicine, Washington University
King, Rosalyn C., Pharm.D., M.P.H., Director, International Health Institute, Charles R. Drew University of Medicine and Science
Klein, Gordon, M.D., Associate Professor of Pediatrics and Human Nutrition, University of Texas Medical Branch, Pediatric Gastroenterology Division
Kolata, Gina, Science Writer, *The New York Times*
Lasagna, Louis, M.D., Dean, Sackler School of Graduate Biomedical Science, Tufts University
Layloff, Thomas P., Ph.D., Director, Division of Drug Analysis, Food and Drug Administration

Leighton, Charles C., M.D., Senior Vice President Administration, Planning & Science Policy, Merck Research Laboratories
Levy, Robert I., M.D., President, Wyeth-Ayerst Research
Marcus, Carol S., Ph.D., M.D., Director, Nuclear Medicine Outpatient Clinic, Harbor-UCLA Medical Center
Martin, Gail, Editor, Editorial Associates
Masica, Suzanne, Graphics Facilitator
McDonald, Michael, M.P.H., President, Windom Health Enterprises
McGinnis, Diane, Assistant Executive Director, Practitioner Reporting Programs, U.S. Pharmacopeial Convention, Inc.
Mollica, Joseph A., Ph.D., President & CEO, DuPont Merck Pharmaceutical Company
Monaco, Grace Powers, J.D., Director, Medical Care Ombudsman Program, Medical Care Management, Inc.
Northup, Sharon C., Ph.D., Research Director, Director of Toxicology, Baxter Healthcare Corporation
Novitch, Mark, M.D., Vice Chairman, The Upjohn Company
Reinders, Thomas P., Pharm.D., Director of Pharmacy Services/Assistant Dean, Medical College of Virginia, Virginia Commonwealth University
Schondelmeyer, Stephen, Pharm.D, Ph.D., Professor and Director, PRIME Institute, College of Pharmacy, University of Minnesota
Shangraw, Ralph F., Ph.D., Professor, Department of Pharmaceutics, School of Pharmacy, University of Maryland
Somers, Emmanuel, Ph.D., Director General, Drugs Directorate, Health and Welfare Canada, Health Protection Branch
Strang, J. Robert, Director of Operations, U.S. Pharmacopeial Convention, Inc.
Trachtenberg, Alan I., M.D., M.P.H., Medical Officer, Science Policy & Analysis Branch, National Institute on Drug Abuse, Office of Science Policy, Education & Legislation
Ullman, Dana, M.P.H., President, Homeopathic Educational Services
Valentino, Joseph G., J.D., Associate Executive Director, U.S. Pharmacopeial Convention, Inc.
Vodra, William W., J.D., Partner, Arnold & Porter
Walson, Philip D., M.D., Professor Pediatrics, Pharmacology, Pharmacy, and Allied Health Services, The Ohio State University
Yarbro, John W., M.D., Ph.D., Medical Director, Regional Cancer Center, Memorial Medical Center

Index

A

B

C

D

E

F

G

H

I

J

K

L

M

N

O

P

Q

R

S

T

U

V

W

Y